ITALO CALVINO
and the Landscape of Childhood

ITALIAN PERSPECTIVES

SERIES EDITORS
Z. G. Barański & A. L. Lepschy

In the light of growing academic interest in Italy and the re-organization of many university courses in Italian along interdisciplinary lines, this book series aims to bring together different scholarly perspectives on Italy and its culture.

Italian Perspectives publishes books and collections of essays on any aspect and period of Italian literature, language, history, culture, politics, art, and media, as well as studies which take an interdisciplinary approach and are methodologically innovative. The series welcomes books written in English and in Italian.

PREVIOUSLY PUBLISHED:

1. *The Letters of Giacomo Leopardi 1817–1837.* Selected and translated by Prue Shaw. 1998; vi + 296 pp. ISBN 0 901286 97 4
2. *Nelle* Carceri *di G. B. Piranesi 1817–1837.* Silva Gavuzzo-Stewart. 1999; viii + 160 pp. ISBN 0 902653 00 9
3. *Speculative Identities: Contemporary Italian Women's Narrative.* Rita Wilson. 2000; viii + 200 pp. ISBN 1 902653 13 0
4. *Elio Vittorini: The Writer and the Written.* Guido Bonsaver. 2000; x + 262 pp. ISBN 1 902653 14 9
5. *Origin and Identity: The Essays of Suevo and Trieste.* Elizabeth Schächter. 2000; viii + 184 pp. ISBN 1 902653 12 2

ITALO CALVINO and the Landscape of Childhood

Claudia Nocentini

NORTHERN
UNIVERSITIES
PRESS
2000

ITALIAN PERSPECTIVES 6

Published by Northern Universities Press,
an imprint of W. S. Maney & Son Ltd,
Hudson Road, Leeds LS9 7DL, UK.
Telephone: +44 (0)113 249 7481
Fax: +44 (0)113 248 6983

ISBN: 1 902653 23 8
ISSN: 1464–1879

Produced in Great Britain by Maney Publishing, Leeds

We gratefully acknowledge the contribution of the Italian Cultural Institute in London towards the publication of this volume.

Front cover: A sketch by Calvino himself illustrating *Il barone rampante* first published in *Notiziario Einaudi* in June 1957.

Back cover: First page of the manuscript of *Il barone rampante* first published in *Album Calvino.*

Contents

Acknowledgements *page vi*

Introduction *1*

CHAPTER I The Realist Landscape *11*

'Uomo nei gerbidi' *13*

Il sentiero dei nidi di ragno 18

'La casa degli alveari' *27*

L'entrata in guerra 31

CHAPTER II The Landscape of the Fairy-Tale *39*

CHAPTER III Echo Effects *49*

'La formica argentina' *52*

Il barone rampante 57

La speculazione edilizia 62

CHAPTER IV The Inner Landscape *67*

I giovani del Po 68

La strada di San Giovanni 71

'La spirale' *77*

'Il conte di Montecristo' *81*

'Dall'opaco' *84*

Le città invisibili 88

Se una notte d'inverno un viaggiatore 93

Bibliography *101*

Index *106*

Acknowledgements

My thanks go to the many friends, colleagues and students who, with their interest and their objections, helped me clarify the ideas and argument contained in this book.

Anna Laura Lepschy has provided the precious guidance, encouragement and support without which this work would not have been possible. Patrizia Molteni has been a constantly available adviser, critic and troubleshooter.

I am also grateful to Claudio Barenghi, David Bellos, Giorgio Bertone, Isa Busticardi, Gianni Celati, Gabriel Josipovici, Giulio Lepschy, Rita Manzini, Martin McLaughlin, Guido Neri, Natalie Roelens, Emanuela Tandello, Michael Wood and John Woodhouse for their specialist help and advice.

John Barnes and the anonymous readers of the Dublin Foundation made very useful suggestions; Judith Landry and Jenny Lowe helped with the translation and linguistic revision of the manuscript, and David Hurrel with cybernetic competence.

Finally, I would also like to acknowledge the contribution of the Dean of Arts' research fund of the University of Edinburgh.

Introduction

Superlatives should be used sparingly, but they are unavoidable when describing Italo Calvino's standing within the post-war period in Italy. From 1946, the date of his first novel, to 1985, the date of his death, Calvino was one of the most active contributors to the emergence of a democratic culture in Italy, both with his work as an editor for the influential publishing house Einaudi, and with his own creative writing which has delighted a wide audience of readers. Calvino is arguably the most versatile, fascinating and inspiring writer of those years.

Calvino's popularity in Italy owes much to the fact that he filled a cultural gap by providing stimulating and intelligent narratives for young teenagers, very different from the outmoded Italian products with which they were fed or the foreign literature in translation on which they had come to rely. His fiction has succeeded in merging didacticism and entertainment so that some of his books, such as *Marcovaldo* and *Il barone rampante*, have become ideal reading material in early secondary education, thus widening his readership and often creating an affectionate bond between the author and his Italian audience.[1] On the other hand, the complexity of social and cultural issues which forms the basis of his writing, the tantalizing network of literary, scientific and historical references, the dazzling clarity and wit of his prose are a challenge to all readers.

From 1946 to 1985, Calvino's witty and sophisticated presence on the Italian literary scene revealed itself in a subtle manner; his very reserved, modest and self-effacing behaviour concealed what has come to be seen as a contribution of the highest order. Since he shunned a visible and central role in Italian society and culture he had more freedom to explore in depth what lay outside the national borders. Calvino travelled extensively and lived in Paris for sixteen years (1964–1980), only going back to Italy for the last five years of his life. Such genuine cosmopolitanism is perhaps what has helped him to achieve a wide readership outside Italy. His works have been widely translated and are also studied in universities throughout the world.

For an introductory evaluation of Calvino's style it is useful to consider the end of the first chapter of *Se una notte d'inverno un viaggiatore*, where an anonymous Reader is holding a book by Calvino also entitled *Se una notte d'inverno un viaggiatore*, which he is beginning

[1] For information about Calvino's interest in the educational field see P. Giovannetti, 'Calvino, la scuola e l'editoria scolastica: l'idillio dimezzato' and I. Bezzera Violante, '«La lettura»: Calvino e un'antologia per la scuola media inferiore' in *Calvino e l'editoria*, edited by L. Clerici and B. Falcetto (Milan, Marcos Y Marcos, 1993), pp. 35–82 and pp. 83–94.

to read. The narrating voice describes the reactions of the Reader to the book's initial impact:

> Ecco dunque ora sei pronto ad attaccare le prime righe della prima pagina. Ti prepari a riconoscere l'inconfondibile accento dell'autore. No. Non lo riconosci affatto. Ma, a pensarci bene, chi ha mai detto che questo autore ha un accento inconfondibile? Anzi, si sa che è un autore che cambia molto da libro a libro. E proprio in questi cambiamenti si riconosce che è lui.
>
> (*Romanzi e racconti* II, 619)[2]

These changes in tone are probably the characteristic which we find most fascinating in Calvino, and indeed the aim of the present study is to pay tribute to its variety. The decision to examine the successive reworkings of the landscape pattern of sea–city–hills, a somewhat marginal element of the surface structure, provided me with the link between works ranging from Neorealist to Post-Modern, and between characters as diverse as Resistance fighters, crusaders, Marco Polo and unicellular organisms.

The descriptive motif is linked to a biographical one: it is a literary representation of the landscape of Sanremo, in the north-western region of Liguria, where Calvino spent most of his childhood, his entire adolescence and his early youth.

The pattern sea–city–hills appears in sixteen works written over a period of thirty-two years. Yet the name, Sanremo, is mentioned only once in his fiction and the reader has to watch closely for the recurrence of the pattern to be able to recognize the topography of the place. Calvino disguises it in a variety of ways, first of all by leaving it unnamed. This happens in 'La formica argentina', where the landscape pattern is clearly marked, but the name of the place is omitted. A slightly higher degree of openness is the mention of the name Riviera in *La speculazione edilizia*, but it refers to the region rather than to a specific town, and the town in question is designated by three asterisks. Finally, names can be changed altogether and the new name brought into line with other characteristics of the narrative, so that Ombrosa is the fitting name for the city dominated by trees in *Il Barone Rampante*, and something as foreign-sounding as Pëtkwo is well-suited to a 'Cimmerian' resort in *Se una notte d'inverno un viaggiatore*.

Since names cannot be trusted, my analysis relies on the recurrence of a landscape which can be broken down into a pattern of sea–city–hills, and takes as its starting point a preliminary subdivision of the material according to criteria of representation, or rather of representational distortion, applied to this landscape. I have singled out four types of representation which form the basis for this book's division into chapters.

I have defined the landscape of the first chapter as 'realist' without in any way wishing to suggest that the treatment of the landscape of Sanremo was a faithful copy of reality in the works studied. Indeed, right from the start the freedom with which, by his own admission, the author treated his material will be stressed and how for example he turned those elements in the countryside of which he did not approve into the treacherous spots which the partisans fear to cross in *Il sentiero dei nidi di ragno*. Thus by 'realist' we should

[2] I. Calvino, *Romanzi e racconti*, edited by C. Milanini, M. Barenghi and B. Falcetto, 3 vols (Milan, Mondadori, 1991, 1992 and 1994), II, 619.

understand a relationship that is more directly linked to the roots of the narrative convention which goes by the name of nineteenth-century realism. This is a convention in which landscape has a clearly defined role and function as a setting within which the action occurs, with isolated moments of lyricism in which a character, who may also be the narrator, turns his attention to those further or wider areas which normally remain indefinite and with which he cannot establish any direct contact. I believe that this definition covers the landscape in 'Uomo nei gerbidi', *Il sentiero dei nidi di ragno* and *L'entrata in guerra*, both for its value as a stage on which the action takes place, and for its inner personal implications. Indeed, in the 1964 preface to *Il sentiero dei nidi di ragno* Calvino states that this landscape constituted his starting point and gave him his very personal tone vis-à-vis other works of the time.

He noted in the preface that the Italian writers generally known as neorealists, following the example of the American writers of the 1930s, had been inspired by the great variety of landscape and dialects of the different regions of Italy brought into mutual contact by the experience of the Second World War; and that these same writers had found a common starting point in three books of their predecessors Verga, Vittorini and Pavese:

> Ci eravamo fatta una linea, ossia una specie di triangolo: *I Malavoglia, Conversazione in Sicilia, Paesi tuoi*, da cui partire, ognuno sulla base del proprio lessico locale e del proprio paesaggio. [...]
>
> Il mio paesaggio era qualcosa di gelosamente mio (è di qui che potrei cominciare la prefazione riducendo al minimo il cappello di «autobiografia d'una generazione letteraria», entrando subito a parlare di quello che mi riguarda direttamente, forse potrò evitare la genericità, l'approssimazione...), un paesaggio che nessuno aveva mai scritto davvero. (Tranne Montale — sebbene egli fosse dell'altra Riviera — Montale che mi pareva di poter leggere quasi sempre in chiave di memoria locale, nelle immagini e nel lessico). Io ero della Riviera di Ponente; dal paesaggio della mia città — San Remo — cancellavo polemicamente tutto il litorale turistico — lungomare con palmizi, casinò, alberghi, ville — quasi vergognandomene; cominciavo dai vicoli della Città vecchia, risalivo per i torrenti, scansavo i geometrici campi dei garofani, preferivo le «fasce» di vigna e d'oliveto coi vecchi muri a secco sconnessi, m'inoltravo per le mulattiere sopra i dossi gerbidi, fin su dove cominciano i boschi di pini, poi i castagni e così ero passato dal mare — sempre visto dall'alto, una striscia tra due quinte di verde — alle valli tortuose delle Prealpi liguri.
>
> Avevo un paesaggio. Ma per poterlo rappresentare occorreva ch'esso diventasse secondario rispetto a qualcos'altro: a delle persone, delle storie.
>
> (*Romanzi e racconti* I, 1187–88)

In his early work Calvino recreates the landscape around Sanremo censoring its unpleasant aspects. But this is nonetheless a highly mimetic process, from which the Ligurian landscape emerges as a recognizable entity.

The landscape which figures in *Il visconte dimezzato*, the only 'fairy-tale' work examined in the second chapter, is also linked to the convention of the genre. Here my analysis aims to bring out those elements which characterize it as a Ligurian landscape, albeit quite implicitly, given that the landscape of fairy-tales is, by convention, universal.

The possibility afforded by landscape distortion, through the emphasis of a single element, emerges particularly clearly in the third chapter, which looks at works linked to widely differing genres, as 'La formica argentina', *La speculazione edilizia* and *Il barone rampante*. In these the author's descriptive procedure concerning the landscape is basically the same, and has the effect of modifying the pattern as a whole, through the precise attention focused on one of its parts. Thus the landscape which should constitute a novelty for the narrator of 'La formica argentina', is thrust into second place by swarms of invisible ants. Similarly the same landscape pattern sea–city–hills becomes an almost unbroken wooded expanse in *Il barone rampante* and an asphalt jungle in *La speculazione edilizia*.

The landscapes studied in the third chapter are all distorted using the same method, and in this case the method constitutes the madness. The function of the landscape in these works is different from that of the nineteenth-century realist model: rather than a setting within which the action takes place, the landscape, the external world, actually determines its course. Compared with the landscape studied in the first chapter, those which appear in the third are much more obvious projections of the narrating ego. More precisely, they are projections of a fraught relationship between the internal and the external, between the ego and a world in which both parties have become demonized: whereas the 'realist' landscape of the first chapter was multifarious, that of the third is exaggeratedly one-dimensional, and whereas the 'realist' ego of the first chapter had limited scope for action and responsibility, the ego of the third group of works is defined by power and capacity for control. The relationship between ego and landscape is central to this narrative triad. But essentially it is a conventional relationship, one in which both ego and landscape are acting a part — the ego the part of the human being, of everyman, and the landscape that of the world. Outside the sphere of nineteenth-century realism, these three fictions share the same didactic substratum, the same status of *roman à thèse*, put forward as universally valid.

In the fourth chapter I look at works which each use the pattern in a completely different way but which have in common the fact that they treat it as an inner landscape, a starting point in the world, and above all as a place of the imaginary. This is an attitude which Calvino explains indirectly, when he tries to understand the absence in his fiction of the landscape of Paris:

> Da alcuni anni ho una casa a Parigi, e vi passo una parte dell'anno, ma finora questa città non compare mai nelle cose che scrivo. Forse per poter scrivere di Parigi dovrei staccarmene, esserne lontano: se è vero che si scrive sempre partendo da una mancanza, da un'assenza. Oppure esserci più dentro, ma per questo dovrei averci vissuto fin dalla giovinezza: se è vero che sono gli scenari dei primi anni della nostra vita che danno forma al nostro mondo immaginario, non i luoghi della maturità. Dirò meglio: bisogna che un luogo diventi un paesaggio interiore, perché l'immaginazione prenda ad abitare quel luogo, a farne il suo teatro.
>
> (*Romanzi e racconti* III, 102)

In this fourth chapter I analyse the ways in which Calvino reworks the representation of the landscape in depth, because it is here that I look at works such as 'Il conte di Montecristo' in

Ti con Zero and as *Le città invisibili*, where the material has been transformed to such an extent as to make recognition particularly peripheral and uncertain.

The works analysed in the fourth chapter are extremely different, but in them the Sanremo landscape takes on the form of an inner landscape, a landscape of the past. The relationship between ego and landscape has become an annexation of the ego. From a place within which an action unfolds, the landscape becomes a place of reflection, a place where the ego withdraws to meditate upon itself, 'il ritorno e l'immedesimarsi in un paesaggio sempre uguale, specchio di calme riflessioni' (*Saggi* II, 2224).[3] Perhaps it can no longer even be called a place, but a cipher, a symbol whose various values are explored as they arise. From having become mainly an inner landscape, the pattern sea–city–hills once again becomes recognizable as the Ligurian coast from the descriptive and visual point of view. This is so at least for *I giovani del Po, La strada di San Giovanni*, 'La Spirale' and 'Dall'opaco'; and also, slightly less precisely, in *Le città invisibili* and 'Il conte di Monte Cristo'. But there continue to be differences between one landscape and another which are directly related to the various camouflages of the narrating ego, disguised alternatively as a mollusc, a fourteenth-century traveller or a hero of nineteenth-century popular fiction. But these disguises no longer have the function simply of making the landscape different, or less recognizable or less monotonous for the reader: now they generate new narrative possibilities in the exploration of the individual's past.

Moreover, the relationship between the ego and inner landscape may be considered a universal relationship. It is legitimate to suppose that all individuals have their own particular childhood landscape. It may be Venice for Marco Polo (just as it is Florence for Dante, etc.). By extension the relationship may also be projected on to the fictitious characters: Marseilles for Edmond Dantès (or, for instance, London for Moll Flanders, etc.). This time, Calvino's decision to put himself in others' clothing also emphasizes the literary nature of his intent, the self-referential irony of the text. All this seems highly transgressive, but it is in fact only so in the sense in which parody has always been transgressive: in this case too we may speak of convention, of a taste for parody which now goes by the name of post-modern.

Particularly striking among the other inner landscapes are the more directly autobiographical ones, which are attempts to proceed from the universal to the personal: that is, the one when Calvino talks of himself and his youth, and of the cluster of memories linked to the countryside around Sanremo as seen when going up the hills with his father in *La strada di San Giovanni*, and that of Calvino as the 'writing ego' looking out over the inner landscape and darkness in 'Dall'opaco'. These two attempts at 'honest' autobiography also are limited by convention. The first might be said to use a convention of the language of psychoanalytical self-analysis, and the second that of falling into a referential vicious circle which attempts to distinguish the person 'who lives' from the person 'who writes'. And perhaps because even these two autobiographical attempts do not succeed in containing and explaining everything, by means of another jump in level of the self-referential irony, we find a further reworking of the pattern in *Se una notte d'inverno un viaggiatore*. This time the variant consists of rotating the orientation by 180 degrees, and we also have a cold Nordic

[3] I. Calvino, *Saggi*, edited by C. Milanini, M. Barenghi and B. Falcetto, 2 vols (Milan, Mondadori, 1995), II, 2224.

landscape, strewn with symbols already encountered in previous appearances of the landscape.

If the constant of this group of works is the inward nature of the landscape, the novelty of the works dealt with in this fourth chapter is their introspective quality. Calvino's self-questioning concerning the landscape, his rereading of it in a psychological-autobiographical vein, allows and at the same time enforces a rereading in the same vein of the previous works. Thus for example, in the light of the information contained in *La strada di San Giovanni,* we understand more clearly the remoteness of the paternal figure and the centrality of the search for the father in the works analysed in the first chapter. The works analysed in the second and the third chapters, on the other hand, could all be reread not only as variations of the conflict between ego-landscape and individual-world, but also as individual-family-world. In this case it is revealing to note how remoteness is, if not completely reassessed, at least seen in a more favourable light; one might then infer that these narratives mark the stages of a reassessment and possibly an understanding of the paternal attitude. Moreover, the return of the Sanremo landscape and the relationship with the family in the group of stories analysed in the second and third section of this study bear out the impossibility of detaching morals from personal and family experience.

The material of each chapter has been subdivided on the basis of criteria of representation. The works are studied in chronological order based on the dates of first publication, with the aim of reconstructing a hypothetical discourse, with the landscape as its ideal protagonist, by pinpointing themes which Calvino links to this same background.[4] It is worth noting at this juncture that one of the most important of these is his ambivalent relation to Sanremo. In reply to Maria Corti's question concerning the places which he had found most congenial and stimulating, Calvino replied with a paradox:

> La città che ho sentito come la mia città più di qualunque altra è New York. Una volta ho perfino scritto, imitando Stendhal, che volevo che sulla mia tomba fosse scritto 'newyorkese'.
>
> (*Saggi* II, 2925)

4 I have not found other studies of this recurrence, though it has been noted by several critics. It is referred to briefly in the biography by E. Mondello, *Italo Calvino* (Pordenone, Edizioni Studio Tesi, 1990), more extensively in L. Barcanelli and E. Faviero, *Album Calvino* (Milan, Mondadori, 1995), and, for the landscape in *La speculazione edilizia, Il barone rampante* and *Le città invisibili,* in M. Quaini, 'La Sanremo di Italo Calvino', in *Italo Calvino la letteratura, la scienza, la città,* edited by G. Bertone (Genova, Marietti, 1988), pp. 60–66. Adopting an almost anthropological point of view Nava gives a short study of spaces in Calvino's fiction in 'La geografia di Calvino', paper delivered at the *Convegno internazionale di studi sull'opera di Calvino,* Florence, 26–28 February 1987. More recently, the importance of this landscape is noted by the editors of *Romanzi e racconti, I saggi* and *Album Calvino.* The main arguments of this book was briefly sketched in my own 'Il paesaggio ricorrente nella narrativa di Calvino' in *The Bulletin of the Society for Italian Studies,* 20 (1987), pp. 13–22, and an earlier version of my analysis of *Le città invisibili* was published as 'La San Remo invisibile di Calvino' in *The Italianist,* 9 (1989), pp. 79–88. The most recent studies on Calvino, including M. McLaughlin, *Italo Calvino* (Edinburgh, University Press, 1998), C. Benedetti, *Pasolini contro Calvino* (Turin, Bollati Boringhieri, 1998) and the analysis of the debate it generated by R. Gordon, 'Pasolini contro Calvino: culture, the canon and the millennium', *Modern Italy,* 3 i (1998), pp. 87–99, S. Chessa Wright, *La poetica neobarocca in Calvino* (Ravenna, Longo, 1998) and C. Benussi, *Scrittori di terra, di mare, di città* (Milan, Nuova Pratiche, 1998) are not discussed here as they appeared in print when the manuscript of this book had been completed. It is my intention to dedicate a comprehensive review article to them at a later date.

And yet, as he also stated in *Eremita a Parigi* (1974), the various cities where he lived — Milan and Turin immediately after the war, New York, for which he expressed such devotion although he lived there only briefly, and Paris, where he moved with his wife and daughter in 1964, to return to Italy and settle in Rome in 1980 — do not figure very large in his writing.

To the question 'Why did the landscape of Sanremo reappear so many times in Calvino's work?', the first and perhaps most relevant answer is the one Calvino himself gave when he said that it is the images that surround us during the first years of life which form the stock-in-trade of the imagination:

> Come ambiente naturale quello che non si può respingere o nascondere è il paesaggio natale e familiare; San Remo continua a saltar fuori nei miei libri nei più vari scorci e prospettive, soprattutto vista dall'alto, ed è soprattutto presente in molte delle *Città invisibili.* Naturalmente parlo di com'era cinquanta o sessanta anni fa, quando ero bambino. Ogni indagine non può che partire da quel nucleo da cui si sviluppano l'immaginazione, la psicologia, il linguaggio; questa persistenza è in me forte quanto era stata forte in gioventù la spinta centripeta la quale presto si rivelò senza ritorno, perché rapidamente i luoghi hanno cessato d'esistere.
>
> (*Saggi* II, 2926)

This passage, with its juxtaposition of the verbs 'respingere', 'nascondere' and 'saltar fuori' and its definition of that force which actually drew him away from Sanremo as a 'spinta centripeta', once again demonstrates his ambiguous and unresolved relationship with the landscape. I have previously quoted the passage from *Eremita a Parigi* (*Romanzi e racconti* III, 102) in which, talking of the places he does not write about because they are too close to him, he recalls that writing always proceeds 'da una mancanza, da una assenza', and the passage in the preface to *Il sentiero dei nidi di ragno* where he says 'il mio paesaggio era qualcosa di gelosamente mio'. The closing words of the quotation above, 'senza ritorno perché rapidamente i luoghi hanno cessato d'esistere', confirm that absence is indeed 'present' here.

It is the necessary experience of loss which sparks off the imagination. And, if we bear in mind that 'immaginazione' and 'fantasia' are one and the same for Calvino, we might recall another of his paradoxes: 'la fantasia è un posto dove ci piove dentro', an observation which gives rise to the penultimate of the *Lezioni americane*, devoted to visibility:[5]

[5] The visual nature of the memories of childhood and their connection with loss has been noted by many writers, for example see Salman Rushdie: 'It may be that writers in my position, exiles or emigrants or expatriates, are haunted by some sense of loss, some urge to reclaim, to look back, even at the risk of being mutated into pillars of salt. But if we do look back, we must also do so in the knowledge — which gives rise to profound uncertainties — that our physical alienation from India almost inevitably mean that we will not be capable of reclaiming precisely the thing that was lost; that we will, in short create fictions, not actual cities or villages, but invisible ones, imaginary homelands, Indias of the mind' in S. Rushdie, *Imaginary Homelands* (London, Granta Books and Viking Penguins, 1991), p. 10. The resilience with which these images keep reappearing has also been noted, see for example Montale: 'È curioso pensare che ognuno di noi ha un paese come questo, e sia pur diversissimo, che dovrà restare il suo paesaggio, immutabile; è curioso che l'ordine fisico sia così lento a filtrare in noi e poi così impossibile a scancellarsi', E. Montale, 'Dov'era il tennis...' (1943), in *La bufera e altro* (Milan, Mondadori, 1957), pp. 48–49.

> Da dove «piovono» le immagini nella fantasia? Dante aveva giustamente un alto concetto di se stesso, tanto da non farsi scrupolo di proclamare la diretta ispirazione divina delle sue visioni. Gli scrittori più vicini a noi, (tranne qualche raro caso di vocazione profetica) stabiliscono collegamenti con emittenti terrene, come l'inconscio individuale o collettivo, il tempo ritrovato nelle sensazioni che riaffiorano dal tempo perduto, le epifanie o concentrazioni dell'essere in un singolo punto o istante. Insomma si tratta di processi che anche se non partono dal cielo esorbitano dalle nostre intenzioni e dal nostro controllo, assumendo rispetto all'individuo una sorta di trascendenza.
>
> (*Saggi* I, 702)

By containing a reference to the landscape of Sanremo, each of these works bears a visible autobiographical mark, the sign of a specific experience. These very reasons, the centrality of the eye and the visual in Calvino's fiction on the one hand, and his protective and at the same time detached attitude towards privacy on the other, make the landscape a motif of evident importance in his narrative style. The reasons for the masking and reworking of these same inner landscapes are many and harder to determine. The most apparent reason is the avoidance of regionalism to which a more recognizable association would point, as already stated in 'Il midollo del leone' in 1950:

> Oggi è al romanzo e al racconto invece che viene deputato il compito di rappresentare il «vero volto» di questa o di quella località geografica. Ed è una richiesta sbagliata perché il romanzo vive nella dimensione della storia, non della geografia. Il vero tema d'un romanzo dovrà essere una definizione del nostro tempo, non di Napoli o di Firenze.
>
> (*Saggi* I, 18)[6]

[6] The threat which Calvino perceived in regionalism, was clearly its traditional and regressive aspect: 'È sul «fare storia» che deve puntare lo scrittore, pur sempre partendo dalla realtà del paese che più ama e conosce: e la storia, ci è stato insegnato, è sempre storia contemporanea, è intervento attivo nella storia futura. Si dirà che a puntare su una descrittiva geografico-sociologica non c'è veramente nessuno: gli scrittori più legati ai luoghi cercano nell'espressione d'un sentimento, d'un ritmo di vita che è il segreto accento autoctono. Ma appunto in questo sovrappiù di commozione, in questo bisogno di eccitazione nostalgica è il primo vero rifiuto della storia; non è la commozione, non è il rapporto affettivo lo stato migliore per intendere il mondo d'oggi: siamo anche qui nel vitalismo romantico, nella vaga mistica corale' (*Saggi* I, 19). Much in the same vein, Calvino always rejected the use of dialect as a linguistic feature connected with the poetics of regionalism; on the other hand whilst in 'Il midollo del leone', quoted above, the more intimate dimension of the relationship between writer and landscape is still feared as partly linked with reactionary self-indulgence, these reservations were very short-lived as any of the narratives studied in this book will demonstrate. The following extract from '*Prefazione 1965 all'edizione scolastica del Barone rampante*', written in the third person but by the author himself, proves without doubt that Calvino was well aware that he had changed his mind about it: '*Il paesaggio ligure.* Questo materiale di costruzione di provenienza intellettuale non deve farci dimenticare che il libro nasce da un'immagine legata ai ricordi infantili — il ragazzo che sale sull'albero — cioè ha la sua prima spinta nell'ambito lirico di quella «letteratura della memoria» che occupa tanto posto nella narrativa del Novecento. I momenti di abbandono lirico dell'Autore, anche se rari e sempre controllati, non solo esistono, ma senza di essi il libro non sarebbe probabilmente nato. C'è quasi nascosto dentro il libro, un altro libro più sommesso, di nostalgica evocazione d'un paesaggio, o meglio: di ri-invenzione d'un paesaggio attraverso la composizione, l'ingrandimento, la moltiplicazione di sparsi elementi di memoria. E le pagine lirico-paesaggistiche sono quelle che rivelano una maggiore precisione visiva e linguistica, sono le più elaborate nel senso d'una scrittura musicale, ricca ed esatta' (*Romanzi e racconti* I, 1228).

To a certain extent, another reason for changes to the landscape must have been a desire to avoid repetition; and also that the narrating of lived experience is always distorted by the genres in which it occurs:

> Il libro della mia memoria? No, la memoria è vera finché non la si fissa, finché non la si chiude in una forma.
>
> (*Romanzi e racconti* II, 789)

The final reason for variety is that the world of the imagination is *par excellence* something which cannot be revealed in its entirety, but which can be explored only by means of partial representations.

CHAPTER I

The Realist Landscape

The texts to be studied in this chapter have much in common. First, they were all written within a relatively short space of time, over a period of seven years, between 1946 and 1953. The first three were written in the immediate post-war period when, for the young Calvino, Sanremo was the dramatic setting both for recent events, and for all of his personal experience. In the last two, written after the 1948 political disillusionment of the Italian left, but before Calvino renounced the Communist party after the Soviet military intervention in Hungary, the return to the landscape of Sanremo is linked to the awakening of the author's historical awareness and hence also, in part, the origins of his political opinions.

But the stylistic links between these texts are more interesting than their temporal framework, and this is why they have been chosen. The representations of the Sanremo landscape brought together in this chapter have not moved very far from the conventions of nineteenth-century realism. In these texts as in realist fiction, the landscape has a well defined role and function as a field within which the action occurs, in a mimesis of the relation between subject and space in reality. It also serves roughly to characterize the socio-economic background of the characters, in a deterministic relationship which echoes the presumed interaction between the individual understood as a historical subject, and his or her milieu. Lastly, if we regard reflection on the landscape by any one character (who clearly may also be the narrator) as a particular kind of activity which throws light on his or her state of mind, the external world is also an indicator of emotional concerns. In other words, if it cannot be said that Calvino was doing anything very original stylistically in these texts, they still add to our understanding of his way of proceeding. Moreover, during these years Calvino saw the Ligurian Riviera as a relatively unknown landscape in Italian literature ('un paesaggio che nessuno aveva mai descritto davvero', *Prefazione 1964*, in *Romanzi e racconti* II, 1188), and the very fact of representing it was already proof of originality:

> Sono d'una terra, la Liguria, che d'una tradizione letteraria ha solo frammenti o accenni, cosicché ognuno può — gran fortuna! — scoprirsi o inventarsi una tradizione per suo conto
>
> ('Forestiero a Torino', 1953, in *Saggi* II, 2705)

This is a somewhat surprising statement if we consider Montale's contribution (though he had described the other Riviera, as Calvino specifies in the *Prefazione 1964*), but understandable if seen in relation to the public whom Calvino was addressing, an occasional public such as that of the readers of *L'Unità*, broader and presumably far less specialized than the readers of *Ossi di seppia*.

Here it may be helpful to refer briefly to Calvino's articles on Sanremo and Liguria, published in *Il Politecnico* during this same period — 'Liguria magra e ossuta' (1945), 'Riviera di Ponente' and 'Sanremo città dell'oro' (1946) — as proof of the need to give prominence to a world he considered to be often ignored in the broader national context. The first article analyses the natural and historical causes of the poverty of the local agriculture. The second, 'Riviera di Ponente', provides a brief description of the interconnected course taken by two kinds of local history:

> la storia della Riviera di Ponente si può raccontare in due maniere; una che tratta della storia degli uomini tra loro, del popolo e della piccola borghesia prima contro i saraceni poi contro i nobili, poi contro i vescovi, poi contro i genovesi, poi contro i Savoia, poi contro i fascisti. L'altra che racconta la lotta degli uomini con la terra di come i terreni coltivati a segale o a fave tornarono incolti, di come agli agrumeti succedettero le piantagioni di rose e di garofani, di come gli uliveti deperirono e furono abbandonati e distrutti.[1]

The third one, 'Sanremo città dell'oro', traces the history of the old and poor city of Sanremo, known as la Pigna, and of its mirror image, Sanremo the affluent tourist trap.

The ideological slant of Calvino's vision leaves no room for doubt, but if there was an initial propensity to portray Sanremo as a predominantly peasant backdrop, at once picturesque and unassuming, it was short-lived, particularly since what mattered to Calvino in those years was indeed a vision of involvement in history rather than an interest in rural idylls.

Proof of this tendency remains, above all in works which were later abandoned, such as 'Alba sui rami nudi' and 'Di padre in figlio', where the Ligurian landscape — but only the hill-country, and therefore outside the scope of this study — is purely rural, cocooned in its own time-space system and isolated from the rest of the world as much as, maybe even more than, Aci Trezza in *I Malavoglia*. But these are rarities, excluded from later collections precisely because of their anachronism of style. Overall, Calvino's attitude seems directed towards representing local colour as a starting point for a wider exploration of the world, and more rarely as an isolated rejection of history, part of a self-destructive and asocial attitude which reflects the bizarre exception and not the rule.

The texts studied in this chapter are those in which the landscape appears in its entirety, or rather, as made up of sea-city-hills, and hence only a small part of those which the landscape of Sanremo appears, also in a realist manner but only in part ('I figli poltroni', 'I fratelli Bagnasco', 'Paura sul sentiero' etc.). This limitation also brings with it consequences concerning content, because the greater importance given to the external worlds tends to shed light on the emotional state of the characters who people and contemplate the landscape, restricting their other activities, so that these are among the most meditative and peaceful of the first writings in which the Sanremo landscape appears.

These works also include a representational constant of considerable interest, namely the description of the landscape caught at the moment in which it is touched by light. This concern with the particular instant of perception is undoubtedly one of those stylistic

[1] Italo Calvino, 'Riviera di Ponente', *Il Politecnico*, 21, 16 February 1946.

peculiarities of Calvino's prose which have earned him a reputation as a scientific writer, not in the literal sense, but, once again, in the nineteenth-century understanding of the term, i.e. as a writer capable of capturing and expressing the specificity of a range of natural phenomena concisely and perceptively.

'Uomo nei gerbidi'

The first appearance of the landscape of Sanremo dates from a story of 1946 entitled 'Uomo nei gerbidi'. It is an account of a hare-hunting expedition with the narrator's father, of the route taken to reach the ideal location and of talk with a local peasant and his daughter while his father has gone off to drive the game out of the wood. The hare manages to escape unhurt and the hunt is abandoned. But hunting is merely an excuse for the narrator to reach the preferred position from which to contemplate his panorama. The narrative first person is clearly autobiographical,[2] and one can even recognize a brief portrait of Calvino in the following:

> camminavo a passi lunghi come mio padre ma con le mani seppellite nelle tasche e il lungo collo appollaiato tra le spalle
>
> (*Romanzi e racconti* I, 186)

Equally biographical, from a psychological point of view, is the narrator's singular proneness to imaginative speculation which immediately reveals him as differing from his original milieu:

> Al mattino presto si vede la Corsica: sembra una nave carica di montagne sospesa laggiù sull'orizzonte. Se si fosse in un altro paese ne sarebbero nate delle leggende; da noi no: la Corsica è un paese povero, più povero del nostro, nessuno ci è mai andato e nessuno ci ha mai pensato.
>
> (*Romanzi e racconti* I, 186)[3]

2 Although the figure of the narrator is clearly autobiographical, and although it is included in that section of *I racconti* entitled 'Le memorie difficili', this is not overt biography because we are given no precise information about the author's name, see below p. 73. The distinction strikes me as useful for various reasons. The first is that, when viewed in relation to other texts where the morning outings with his father are described, this story omits significant details. Unlike 'L'occhio del padrone' this text contains no real pointers to the class differences between the family of the narrator and that of Baccinin Beato; while unlike 'La strada di San Giovanni' it does not make explicit the narrator's antipathy for the early risings upon which his father insists. This might be a form of self-censorship, or poetic licence, a sort of masking which, elsewhere, led Calvino to add the fictional character of a sister in 'A pranzo con un pastore', alongside those modelled on the author's family.

3 The narrator of 'Uomo nei gerbidi' is careful not to say what kind of legend might have sprung up in connection with Corsica, but here I think that we may legitimately hazard a guess. In both 'La casa degli alveari' and 'La spirale' in 'Il sangue e il mare' and in *Se una notte d'inverno un viaggiatore*, the sea is associated with death. An island beyond the sea might well be transformed into the isle of the dead, as happens in various legends of the blessed, images of a horizontal beyond, where the barrier between living and dead is made up of the water that separates them. See C. Segre, *Fuori dal mondo: i modelli nella follia e nelle immagini dell'aldilà* (Turin, Einaudi, 1990), pp. 18–19, and C. Ginzburg, *Storia notturna: una decifrazione del sabba* (Turin, Einaudi, 1989), pp. 83–84.

Yet this tendency towards contemplation and day-dreaming has youthful aspects, since it is not without reserve and a certain sense of alarm:

> La Corsica sparì bevuta dalla luce, ma tra mare e cielo il confine non si quagliò: rimase quella zona ambigua e smarrita che fa male guardare perché non esiste.
>
> (*Romanzi e racconti* I, 186)

The description of the landscape dwells mainly upon the moment of perception, as we see right from the first phrase: 'Al mattino presto si vede la Corsica' (*Romanzi e racconti* I, 186) and despite the colloquial register it is predominantly an objective and scientific analysis of the phenomenon:

> Quando di mattina si vede la Corsica è segno che l'aria è chiara e ferma e non accenna a piovere.
>
> (*Romanzi e racconti* I, 186)

At all events, attention is focused on the phenomenon of dawn, the changing and brightening of the colours from that half-light where, although the field of vision was greater, the masses of colour were almost indistinguishable:

> Le cose impigrivano nel grigio dell'alba come in un socchiudere di palpebre ancora assonnate. Al mare non si distinguevano confini, traversato fino in fondo da lame di foschia.
>
> (*Romanzi e racconti* I, 187)

This change is produced by light:

> L'alba andava scoprendo i colori, a uno a uno. Prima il rosso delle bacche [di gigaro], dei tagli zonati sugli alberi di pino. Poi il verde, i cento, i mille verdi dei prati, dei cespugli del bosco, poco prima tutti eguali: adesso invece ogni momento c'era un nuovo verde che nasceva e si distingueva dagli altri. Poi l'azzurro: quello urlante del mare che assordò tutto e fece restare pallido e timoroso il cielo.
>
> (*Romanzi e racconti* I, 187)

The expedient of using an extraneous and incongruous point of reference to describe the dominance of one blue over another, the recourse to words taken from the semantic field of sound, emphasizes the quality of the perception and at the same time increases the magnetic power of the object observed, introducing the sense of dizziness which upsets the observer.

The light is reflected off the sea, it is dazzling. Its task of breaking up the solid, compact mass overlooking it is harder:

> A un tratto case, tetti, vie nacquero a piè delle colline, in riva al mare. Ogni mattina la città nasceva così dal regno delle ombre, tutt'a un tratto, fulva di tegole, baluginante di vetri, calcinosa d'intonachi. La luce ogni mattino la descriveva nei particolari più minuti, raccontava ogni suo andito, enumerava tutte le case.
>
> (*Romanzi e racconti* I, 187)

Illuminating the nearest objects first (the berries of the cuckoo-pint, in the 1958 edition), then the horizon, and after having lingered on the village below — with different speeds — the light now rises:

> Poi veniva su per le colline scoprendo sempre nuovi dettagli: nuove fasce, nuove case. Arrivava in Colla Bella, gialla e gerbida e deserta, e scopriva una casa anche lassù, sperduta, la più alta casa prima del bosco, a un tiro di fucile dal mio fucile, la casa di Baccinin il Beato.
>
> (*Romanzi e racconti* I, 187)

Throughout the description the subject of the action is thus not the observer's gaze, as it will be for example in *Palomar*, but the light. It is by following the light, too, that the narrative can produce the playful leap from the house to the gun and a vividly comic inversion which introduces the equally comic character of Baccinin Beato. The effect is one of alienation on the part of the narrator, whose exaggerated passivity is predominant in his relations with others and seems to be one of the main themes of the story, expressed partly through the illusion of objectivity, and the scientific observation of reality, and partly by following the light and reporting the grievances of the other characters.

The meeting between hunter and peasant is humorous: the low-mimetic key in which all the characters are treated sinks to caricature in the description of Baccinin Beato's extreme thinness:

> Uscì Baccinin: era magro che per vederlo bisognava si mettesse di profilo, se no si vedevano solo i baffi che aveva grigi e spiegati nell'aria.
>
> (*Romanzi e racconti* I, 188)

The same applies to the description of his daughter Costanzina:

> Poteva avere sedici anni, la faccia a forma di oliva, gli occhi, la bocca, le narici a forma di oliva e le treccine giù per le spalle. Anche i seni a oliva doveva avere, tutta d'uno stile, raccolta come una statuetta, selvatica come una capra, le calze di lana ai ginocchi.
>
> (*Romanzi e racconti* I, 189)

The dialogue between the narrator and Baccinin Beato is comic, too: both in its style, made up of reiterative repartee, following the model of Vittorini, though humorous in vein and in its content, a list of the more or less serious misfortunes, which have recently befallen Baccinin. The account is rounded off comically by the escape of the hare, which he does not even see, shifting some of his bad luck onto the narrator.

Far from civilization, a victim of the 'gerbida' nature of the places he lives in (heath, moorland), suspicious of and disheartened by history, Baccinin Beato is a prototype of the ineffectual noble savage. His name, a Ligurian version of Battista, might be a reference to the name of the Calvino family's holding, while his nickname is clearly ironic, since his detachment from the human community, instead of bringing him relief or blessedness, is a source of constant disappointment, and his conversation is a litany of complaints.[4] Realizing that his suggestions are falling upon ground at least as stony as that on which they are standing, the narrator adopts a courteous attitude, comforting on the surface but actually remote.

[4] See 'La strada di San Giovanni', in *Romanzi e racconti* III, 7–26.

> (Baccinin) Scarogna, scarogna. Già io per la lepre non ci sono portato. Preferisco mettermi sotto un pino e aspettare i tordi. In una mattina cinque o sei botte si sparano.
> (Narratore) — Così vi fate la pietanza, Baccinin Beato.
> — Già. Io poi li sbaglio tutti, però.
> — Succede. Le cartucce, sono.
> — Cartucce, cartucce.
> — Quelle che vendono sono imbrogli. Caricatevele da voi.
> — Già io me le carico da me, però. Forse le carico male.
> — Eh, bisogna saperci fare.
> — E già, e già.
>
> (*Romanzi e racconti* I, 188)

Baccinin Beato's isolation is defensive, whereas that of his daughter Costanzina is bemused and almost infantile. Listening to her talk of rustic goings-on, the narrator asks: 'Ti piace abitare a Colla Bella?' (*Romanzi e racconti* I, 189). His question barely conceals a destabilizing intent (otherwise he might have used 'vivere' and not 'abitare' or, indeed, the more direct 'Ti piace Colla Bella?'). The girl answers by listing the advantages of town and country with sedulous impartiality. The narrator's question has inadvertently touched a sore spot for Baccinin Beato: that of the general problem of absorbing the unskilled work-force into urban civilization, a phenomenon giving rise to cases of extreme marginalization and exploitation, as Calvino later describes in *Marcovaldo*. For the moment the phenomenon is barely glimpsed in Baccin's comment:

> — Questa qui non ci ha tanta passione per andare in città, ma all'altra piaceva tanto che non è più tornata.
> — Dov'è adesso?
> — Ma.
>
> (*Romanzi e racconti* I, 190)[5]

The text contains no more on the subject. It is clear, however, that for Baccinin the city represents a world from which he is excluded, a world that has nothing to offer to him except danger. It may be an exaggeration to interpret the failure of the hunting expedition as a sort

[5] See Bruno Falcetto's comment concerning the various drafts of the story for the critical edition of *Ultimo viene il corvo*: 'Nei Racconti Calvino cancella il passo del colloquio con Tancina in cui l'io narrante accenna alle seduzioni notturne della città in un'immagine in cui si intravede l'interno di una casa di tolleranza. A dare piena evidenza alla contrapposizione fra mondo urbano e mondo della collina è sufficiente infatti l'episodio della fuga dell'altra figlia di Baccinin (e poi il quadro era di maniera e dissonante rispetto al paesaggio e all'atmosfera del racconto)' (*Romanzi e racconti* I, 1279). Note also Falcetto's observation that the author had 'cleaned up' various texts for the 1958 edition, in *Romanzi e racconti* I, 1275. The censured passage is the following: '— In città ci sono palazzi foderati di specchi, — raccontai, — con saloni che entrando ti fa l'effetto come di un albero di Natale, sai l'albero di Natale? | — Con candeline appese? | — Con donne nude sul petto e dietro; involte in stoffe di tutti i colori, che si ripetono mille volte negli specchi. | — Bello. Mi ci porti? —' (*Romanzi e racconti* I, 1280). My feeling is that the narrator is referring to urban luxury and wealth, to the world of casinos rather than that of the brothel, because the reference to the Christmas tree, like the previous comment on Tancina's diligence, seems to anchor the dialogue in a relationship between an adult and a young girl, where the explicit reference to sexuality would seem inappropriate.

of mirror-image sign that the hills have nothing to offer to the narrator. But the exaggeration is certainly lessened if the text is seen in relation to 'L'occhio del padrone', written at about the same time, in 1947:

> Il figlio andando rivedeva i colori della vallata, ascoltava i ronzii dei calabroni nei frutteti. Ogni volta che tornava al suo paese, dopo mesi passati a illanguidirsi in città lontane, riscopriva l'aria e l'alto silenzio della sua terra come un richiamo dimenticato d'infanzia e insieme con rimorso. Ogni volta venendo alla sua terra restava come nell'attesa di un miracolo: tornerò e questa volta tutto avrà un significato, il verde che digrada a strisce per la vallata del mio podere, i gesti sempre uguali degli uomini al lavoro, la crescita d'ogni pianta, d'ogni ramo; la rabbia di questa terra prenderà anche me, come mio padre, fino a non potermi più staccare di qui.
>
> (*Romanzi e racconti* I, 193)

Nonetheless the relationship between the peasant and the owner's son is doomed to failure. The use of indirect speech explains all too starkly how things stand: 'Sapeva quello che gli uomini pensavano di lui: il vecchio è matto ma suo figlio è scemo' (*Romanzi e racconti* I, 193).

Later, in an interview in 1960, Calvino was to suggest a definition of his subject-matter based on this unsatisfactory relationship with landed property. It is worth quoting the whole passage as it contains an obvious reflection of that passion usually censured in Calvino's fiction:

> Bisogna partire sempre da ciò che si è. La critica sociologica, invece di muoversi nel generico come fa, potrebbe fare questo di concreto; definire dal suo punto di vista la vera essenza d'ogni scrittore, scoprire il suo vero background sociale che magari contrasta con le apparenze. Di me potrebbero forse scoprire che sotto, gratta gratta, c'è il piccolo proprietario di campagna, l'individualista, duro al lavoro, avaro, nemico allo Stato e al fisco, che per reagire a un'economia agricola non redditizia e al rimorso di aver lasciato la campagna in mano ai fittavoli, propone soluzioni universali alla sua crisi, il comunismo o la civiltà industriale o la vita deracinée degli intellettuali cosmopoliti, o soltanto il ritrovare sulla pagina l'armonia con la natura perduta nella realtà.
>
> ('Colloquio con Carlo Bo', in *Saggi* II, 2730)

The explanation is convincing provided that we bear in mind that Calvino is speaking as his own critic. For the reader who remembers the delicacy with which the narrator of 'L'uomo nei gerbidi' changes tack in connection with Baccinin's other daughter it is clear that Calvino's reaction to what he calls 'L'economia agricola non redditizia' is only a small part of his refusal to be a landowner. A more important factor is clearly the sense of injustice linked to the concept of property, as the equally autobiographical 'Pranzo con un pastore' (1948) lucidly explains:

> Soffrivo di questo paragonare me e lui, lui che doveva guardare le capre altrui per vivere, e puzzare di ariete, ed era forte da abbattere le querce, e io che vivevo sulle sedie a sdraio, accanto alla radio leggendo libretti d'opera, che presto sarei andato

> all'università, e non volevo mettermi la flanella sulla pelle perché mi faceva prudere la schiena. Le cose che erano mancate a me per essere lui, e quelle che erano mancate a lui per essere me, io le sentivo allora come un'ingiustizia che faceva me e lui due esseri incompleti che si nascondevano, diffidenti e vergognosi, dietro quella zuppiera di minestra.
>
> ('A pranzo con un pastore', in *Romanzi e racconti* I, 209)

Il sentiero dei nidi di ragno

The panorama of 'Uomo nei gerbidi', although apparently objective it is not entirely so: the fact that one can see Corsica is a reference to the panorama of Sanremo, but the narrator has omitted any reference to what he does not like about the town, as he declared in the preface to *Il sentiero dei nidi di ragno*:

> Del paesaggio della mia città — Sanremo — cancellavo polemicamente tutto il litorale turistico — lungomare con palmizi, casinò, alberghi, ville, — quasi vergognandomene.
>
> (*Romanzi e racconti* I, 1188)

He will be able to represent these aspects only in the emotional distortion to which war has subjected them:

> anche le ville, riuscivo a rappresentare ora che le avevo viste requisite e trasformate in corpi di guardia e prigioni: anche i campi di garofani, da quando erano diventati terreni allo scoperto, pericolosi ad attraversare, evocanti uno sgranare di raffiche nell'aria.
>
> (*Romanzi e racconti* I, 1189)

In *Il sentiero dei nidi di ragno* landscape and action are fused: no longer, or not only, a descriptive element and a framework, the landscape is a constant feature because the characters live in it, cross it as they move from one point to another, charging it with vitality and pathos. By stating the various emotions which it aroused in the writer, the 'Prefazione 1964' suggests a reversed reading, according to which the novel's plot is determined by the very personal relation which Calvino had with these places. The plot reifies the author's idiosyncrasies, suggesting danger, conflict and intrigue where the relationship was one of conflict, and safety, positive behaviour and imaginative freedom where it was less fraught. Thus the old city acts as the backdrop from which the protagonist starts out and the wood lends itself to natural discoveries and daydreaming, while the elegant bourgeois villa houses the prison and the fields of carnations immediately arouse panic.

The memorable opening is particularly rich in effects, and seems to suggest that it may be able to dispense with the personality of the narrator;

> Per arrivare in fondo al vicolo, i raggi del sole devono scendere diritti rasente le pareti fredde, tenute discoste a forza d'arcate che traversano la striscia di cielo azzurro carico.
>
> Scendono diritti i raggi del sole, giù per le finestre messe qua e là in disordine sui muri, e cespi di basilico e di origano piantati dentro pentole ai davanzali, e sottovesti

> stese appese a corde: fin giù al selciato, fatto a gradini e a ciottoli, con una cunetta in mezzo per l'orina dei muli.
>
> (*Romanzi e racconti* I, 5)[6]

Repeating the model of a town 'recounted' by the rays of the sun in 'Uomo nei gerbidi', and incorporating elements referring to the senses of touch and smell (leading to Pin's shout in the subsequent paragraph which introduces that of hearing), this opening scene, introducing the reader into the overcrowded poor districts of the city, is as impartial as a stage direction. Like a theatre backdrop gradually lit from above and constructed on the lines of an urban view which was traditional in both the painting of the end of the nineteenth century and in the photography of the early twentieth, the description of the 'theatre' where the action is about to start alludes to a condition of urban poverty in a context revealed as pre-industrial by the clusters of basil and oregano and the telltale signs of the presence of mules. It is thus in character with the profession of Pin, the young protagonist, who is a cobbler and of his sister, a prostitute; both may be classified as belonging to the provincial *lumpen proletariat.*

Only History, that is World War Two, acts as an agent of change. The city, target of repeated bombings, is disfigured by war:

> È una grande formazione da bombardamento, forse qualche città resterà spianata e fumante, sotto il suo volo, mentr'essa scomparirà dietro le nuvole. Pin sente la terra vibrare sotto il rombo e la minaccia delle tonnellate di bombe appese che trasmigrano sopra la sua testa. La Città Vecchia in quel momento si sta svuotando e la povera gente s'accalca nella fanghiglia della galleria. Si sentono dei tonfi cupi, a sud.
>
> (*Romanzi e racconti* I, 97–98)

In contrast with the picturesque beginning, we have a final vision of trench warfare:

> Le impannate delle botteghe sono chiuse. A ridosso dei muri hanno costruito antischeggie di tavole e sacchi di terra.
>
> (*Romanzi e racconti* I, 143)

The vision of a city emptied of inhabitants, who have been evacuated, deported or killed.

[6] Compare the description of the 'Città Vecchia' with that of the 'Pigna' (pinecone) in 'Sanremo città dell'oro' in *Il Politecnico* (1946): 'Fulcro di questo inurbamento era la Pigna, la vecchia Pigna rannicchiata ancora per paura dei pirati, con le case sostenute una addosso all'altra con archi e volte, sempre più aggrovigliata per le aggiunte e gli adattamenti delle successioni ereditarie, sempre più pigiata per le scosse dei terremoti, con le strade ripide e acciottolate piene di sterco di mulo, la Pigna senza fogne, senz'acqua nelle case, buia nelle strade strette' (*Saggi* II, 2371–72). It is interesting to note that the name of the district known as 'la Pigna' appears only once as such in Calvino's fiction in *La strada di San Giovanni,* in *Romanzi e racconti* III, 8. But it does recur frequently as a simile, and on one occasion as a metaphor for enclosure and protective isolation, see *Romanzi e racconti* I, 493. As regards the visual effect of the light of the sun, apart from the passage quoted above from 'Uomo nei gerbidi', we might also notice the resemblance to the opening of 'Buon a nulla': 'Il sole entrava nella via di sbieco, già alto, illuminandola disordinatamente, ritagliando le ombre dei tetti sui muri delle case di fronte, accendendo di barbagli le vetrine agghindate, battendo, sbucato da insospettati spiragli, sul volto dei passanti frettolosi, che si scansavano su marciapiedi affollati' (*Romanzi e racconti* III, 826). 'Buon a nulla' (1945–46) was a project for a novel which became a short story, published under the title 'Come non fui Noè'.

> — Autista! — dice. — Cosa succede di nuovo nel carrugio? E all'osteria?
> Gian guarda agro: — Non sai niente? — chiede.
> — No, — fa Pin. — Cosa c'è? La Bersagliera ha fatto un figlio?
> Gian sputa: — Io non voglio più sentir parlare di quella gente, — dice. — Io mi vergogno d'esserci nato in mezzo. Erano anni che non ne potevo più, di loro, dell'osteria, della puzza di piscio del carrugio ... Eppure ci restavo ... adesso ho dovuto scappare e quasi ringrazio quella carogna che mi ha fatto la spia ...
> — Miscèl il Francese? — chiede Pin.
> — Il Francese è uno. Ma non è lui, la carogna. Fa il doppio gioco, lui, nella brigata nera e con il gap; ancora non ha ben deciso da quale parte stare ...
> — E gli altri? ...
> — Hanno fatto una retata. hanno preso tutti. Ci eravamo appena decisi a fare il gap ... Giraffa l'hanno fucilato ... Gli altri in Germania ... il carrugio s'è quasi svuotato ... È caduta una bomba d'aeroplano vicino alla ringhiera del forno; tutti sono sfollati o vivono nel tunnel ...
>
> (*Romanzi e racconti* I, 127–28)

The situating of the characters vis-à-vis the war is linked to their acting with or without a sense of community; their belonging is the prerequisite of class consciousness. The clash between personal interest and sense of community forms the dividing line on whose basis the young prostitute will be doomed and Pin saved: at the end of the story he puts the Città Vecchia, a place of poverty, exploitation and betrayal, behind him. Not that 'il groviglio delle esistenze umane' (*Saggi* I, 689) is any less problematic elsewhere: in the hills, too, even where people are fighting on the side of History, betrayal and cruelty are not unknown; the protagonist's very loneliness, which might seem to have been ended by the meeting with the protective figure of the partisan, has ambiguous implications, given that the partisan is his sister's executioner.

The story's movement, away from the city to the hill, appears to suggest the protagonist's reclaiming of the natural world as opposed to an urban existence degraded by poverty and exploitation. The hills are the place of direct confrontation with the Other (whether represented by nature or the enemy), in the open, beyond the bounds of the urban setting, a metaphor for rigid class relations.

And yet if, on the level of the plot, the story of Pin is the load-bearing structure of the tale, from the narrative point of view the child character entails a doubling of focus. As we sense from Pin's first appearance on the scene, narrator and character do not coincide: almost of necessity in a realist context, the choice of an anti-hero such as Pin entails a continual process of mediation and reconciliation between character and reader.[7]

The landscape follows this general dichotomy: it is frightening, grotesque, incomprehensible if seen with Pin's eyes and full of lyricism and pathos if described by the narrator.

[7] This may be the phenomenon referred to in one of the first editorial interpretations of the text by Pavese, now published in the critical apparatus of the Meridiani edition, edited by Milanini. 'Inoltre sovente il mondo del ragazzo è rotto da evocazioni che sanno di sintesi lirica adulta (I passi segnati delle pagg. 18, 38, 48, 58, 85) — qui si sostituisce al ragazzo l'autore. Non che la familiarità del ragazzo con donne, brutture, guerra ecc. sia stonata: è stonato il linguaggio che la esprime' (*Romanzi e racconti* I, 1243). It would seem impossible to track down the relevant passages because the manuscript has been lost.

The two voices often appear one beside the other in the moments of greatest tension, as for instance when, with a deep sense of humiliation and uncertainty, Pin comes out of the inn where he has been incited to steal the pistol:

> Pin ora è nel carrugio. È sera e alle finestre si accendono i lumi. Lontano, nel torrente, cominciano a gracidare le rane; di questa stagione i ragazzi stanno la sera appostati intorno ai laghetti, ad acchiapparle. Le rane strette in mano dànno un contatto viscido, sgusciante, ricordano le donne, così lisce e nude.
>
> (*Romanzi e racconti* I, 13–14)

The lens used by Calvino is bifocal, the elegiac one of the narrator which contrasts the group activity of the boys playing and the frogs croaking, and the expressionistic and grotesque one of the solitary Pin who already imagines himself in close contact with the sliminess of the frog. This is an example of what Cesare Cases has ironically named the 'pathos of distance', thus pinpointing how the relationship between the distance and the desirability of the object observed is a constant feature of the treatment of the emotions in Calvino's fiction (Cesare Cases, 1958).[8]

Elsewhere, we find example of data that are more consonant with the biography of the author than with the characterization of the fictional figure, for instance in the description of the prison:

> La prigione è una grande villa di inglesi requisita perché nella vecchia fortezza sul porto i tedeschi hanno piazzato la contraerea. È una villa strana, in mezzo a un parco d'araucarie, che già prima forse aveva l'aria di una prigione, con molte torri e terrazze e camini che girano al vento, e inferriate che già c'erano prima, oltre a quelle aggiunte.
>
> (*Romanzi e racconti* I, 32)

Here the precise botanical terminology referring to a fairly rare species of tree cannot be thought to be that of the semi-literate Pin; but the 'forse' is already sufficient indication that the character himself could never have thought of it.

It is worth noting that 'forse' is also the key word of another character, the 'commissario di brigata' Kim: to counterbalance the extreme clarity with which he expresses himself, it recurs thirteen times in his thoughts, together with other expressions of doubt, with the obliquity of verbs such as 'sembrare' and 'parere', and with the reiterated use of the subjunctive:

> Un giorno forse io non capirò più queste cose, pensa Kim, tutto sarà sereno in me e capirò gli uomini in tutt'altro modo, più giusto, forse. Perchè: forse? Bene, io allora non dirò più forse, non ci saranno più forse in me.
>
> (*Romanzi e racconti* I, 109)

[8] See C. Cases, 'Calvino e il "pathos della distanza"', in *Città aperta*, 7–8 (1958), pp. 33–35 and in *I metodi attuali della critica in Italia*, edited by M. Corti and C. Segre (Turin, Eri/Edizioni Rai Radiotelevisione Italiana, 1970), pp. 53–58. One of the most striking examples of the 'pathos of distance' is the scene describing the bombing of the city see through binoculars (*Romanzi e racconti* I, 98). Il Dritto accused of negligence following the episode of the fire, reacts with an angry *cupio dissolvi*, hoping that his own house might be the first to be bombed. Pin, on the other hand, seems fascinated rather by the binoculars; but a thought is spared for the inhabitants of the Città Vecchia' under bombardment. This scene is reminiscent of 'Irene' in *Le città invisibili*, in *Romanzi e racconti* II, 463–64.

Kim, the protagonist of the anomalous Chapter IX, is a character who stands apart from the others by virtue of his bourgeois condition, here experienced as a source of friction.[9] He is also responsible for overseeing the work of the resistance fighters, and does not forget them even for a moment when he is alone with his nightly imaginings; indeed, passing from free indirect speech to interior monologue, he wonders about their future after the end of the war (*Romanzi e racconti* I, 108). Both from the point of view of social characterization and from that of his commitment, the figure of Kim follows that of the anonymous narrator. If, from the point of view of content, Calvino described Chapter IX as a sort of 'prefazione inserita in mezzo al romanzo' (*Romanzi e racconti* I, 1189), from the narrative point of view this jump from the level of the plot itself to that of reflection on the plot is a first and explicit foretaste of the *mise-en-abîme.*

Thinking of Kim as the personification in the work of the implied narrator, it may be helpful to note that his reflections surface in the text amidst the shadows of a night walk, hence 'd'int'ubagu', in a landscape shrouded by darkness and mist:[10]

> La valle è piena di nebbie e Kim cammina su per una costiera sassosa come sulle rive di un lago. I larici escono dalle nuvole come pali per attraccare le barche.
>
> (*Romanzi e racconti* I, 111)

Mist, an unequivocal symbol of uncertainty in the text, pervades the whole chapter right from the beginning:

> Verso sera arrivano il comandante Ferriera e il commissario Kim. Fuori salgono voli di nebbia come porte sbattute una dopo l'altra
>
> (*Romanzi e racconti* I, 99)

to the end:

> Alle volte camminando nella notte le nebbie degli animi si condensano intorno, come le nebbie dell'aria
>
> (*Romanzi e racconti* I, 111)

Above all, by considering Kim as a personification of the implied narrator working 'd'int'ubagu' amidst ghostly greyish colours, we have a better understanding of all the references to the violent light, which alarms Pin or hurts his eyes.

> A un tratto le penombre del parco si diradano ed ecco aprirsi ai loro occhi uno scenario luminoso, a colori vivissimi, come quando si scopre una decalcomania. Hanno un movimento di paura e subito si gettano a terra.
>
> (*Romanzi e racconti* I, 45–46)

> Quando Pin si sveglia vede i ritagli di cielo tra i rami del bosco, chiari che fa quasi male guardarli.
>
> (*Romanzi e racconti* I, 55)

[9] From Falcetto's edition we learn that right from his first review of the book, Pavese criticized the basic stylistic incongruity of Chapter IX, where the ideological framework is set out, see *Romanzi e racconti* I, 1244; Vittorini expressed basically the same view, see *Romanzi e racconti* I, 1246–47.

[10] See *Dall'opaco,* in *Romanzi e racconti* III, 101.

> È un giorno azzurro come gli altri, che fa paura vederlo così azzurro
>
> (*Romanzi e racconti* I, 116)

> Il mare che ieri era un torbido fondo di nuvola ai margini del cielo, si fa una striscia d'un cupo sempre più denso ed ora è un grande urlo azzurro al di là d'una balaustra di colline e di case
>
> (*Romanzi e racconti* I, 141)[11]

Night can be even more alarming, but in a different way. Light calls forth an instinctive fear, a more immediate, physical foreboding of death, while darkness causes mysterious 'paure bambine' to resurface, fears which have their roots in blood, as in the recalling of explicitly Freudian primary scenes: [12]

> Pin sale per il carrugio, già quasi buio; e si sente solo e sperduto in quella storia di sangue e corpi nudi che è la vita degli uomini.
>
> (*Romanzi e racconti* I, 14)

> Allora le ombre del ripostiglio si trasformano in sogni strani, di corpi che s'inseguono, si picchiano e s'abbracciano nudi, finché viene qualcosa di grande e caldo e sconosciuto, che sovrasta su di lui, Pin, e lo carezza e lo tiene nel caldo di sé, e questo è la spiegazione di tutto, un richiamo lontanissimo di felicità dimenticata.
>
> (*Romanzi e racconti* I, 16)

Darkness also brings with it a sense of protection, conducive to abandonment and tenderness, a greater ability to be kind, at one with nature. Here, then, we have a scene from a 'fiaba di bosco' as the book was defined by Pavese (1962, p. 268):[13]

> Pin esce da dietro il serbatoio: il gracidare delle rane nasce da tutta l'ampia gola del cielo, il mare è una spada luccicante nel fondo della notte. L'essere all'aperto gli dà un senso di piccolezza che non è paura. Ora Pin è solo, solo su tutto il mondo.

[11] In his analysis of these same descriptive passages Milanini notes that they are all represented in a sort of close-up which never includes the horizon: 'a ricordarci che la nostra conoscenza del reale è sempre parziale e precaria, che la nostra aspirazione alla totalità è tenuta ad esprimersi mediante rappresentazioni circoscritte e tendenziali', in C. Milanini, *L'utopia discontinua: Saggio su Italo Calvino* (Milan, Garzanti 1990), p. 14.

[12] The text's obvious psychoanalytical allusions — the primal scene, Pin's interest in his own excrement — are further proof of the basic affinity between the implied narrator and Kim: 'Kim è studente, invece: ha un desiderio enorme di logica di sicurezza sulle cause e gli effetti, eppure la sua mente s'affolla a ogni istante d'interrogativi irrisolti. C'è un enorme interesse per il genere umano in lui: per questo studia medicina, perché sa che la spiegazione di tutto è in quella macina di cellule in moto, non nelle categorie della filosofia. Il medico dei cervelli, sarà: uno psichiatra: non è simpatico agli uomini perché li guarda sempre fissi negli occhi come volesse scoprire la nascita dei loro pensieri, e a un tratto esce con domande a bruciapelo, domande che non c'entrano niente, su di loro, sulla loro infanzia' (*Romanzi e racconti* I, 99). On the psychoanalytical connotations of the text see also L. Re, *Calvino and the Age of Neorealism: Fables of Estrangement* (Stanford California, Stanford University Press, 1990), especially pp. 256–319.

[13] C. Pavese, 'Il sentiero dei nidi di ragno', in *La letteratura americana e altri saggi* (Turin, Einaudi, 1962), pp. 267–70.

> E cammina per i campi coltivati a garofani e a calendule. Cerca di tenersi alto sul declivio delle colline, per passar sopra alla zona dei Comandi. Poi scenderà al fossato: là sono i suoi luoghi.
>
> Ha fame: di quest'epoca sono mature le ciliege. Ecco un albero, distante da ogni casa: che sia sorto lì per incantesimo? Pin si arrampica tra i rami e comincia a sfrondarli con diligenza. Un grosso uccello gli piglia il volo quasi tra le mani: era lì che dormiva. Pin si sente amico di tutti, in quel momento, e vorrebbe non averlo disturbato.
>
> (*Romanzi e racconti* I, 51)

But night also reawakens dormant tales of horror which inspire fear:

> Sotto il casolare i boschi diradano in strisce di prato, e là dicono che ci sono spie seppellite e Pin ha un po' paura a passarci la notte, per non sentirsi tirare i calcagni da mani cresciute in mezzo all'erba.
>
> (*Romanzi e racconti* I, 69)

This presentiment will come true with the grotesque joke played by Il Dritto, who tricks him into discovering a corpse (*Romanzi e racconti* I, 79). Night is thus the domain of the imaginary, the unexpected, it contains enchanted gardens and gothic novels: every gesture (like shooting at the spiders' dens) may take on incongruous and magical proportions, every encounter (for instance the two meetings with Cugino, which both occur at night) proves to be an essential part of the plot of that personal fairy story which Pin tells himself.

In his review of *Il sentiero dei nidi di ragno*, Pavese wrote that 'la guerra partigiana diventa favola di bosco' (Pavese, p. 268), that is, the micro-story of Pin is inscribed within the macro-story of the war and, in its way, interprets it. The plot of Pin's adventures, like a fairy story about loneliness and how to conquer it, has as its purpose the search for a friend, just as the partisans' war is described in terms of the search for allies, for associative values where personal struggle becomes collective struggle.

To be able to recognize his own friends is Pin's main concern, though in one way or another he remains disappointed until his second meeting with Cugino; thus I cannot fully agree with Falaschi's otherwise convincing interpretation:

> per la verità Pin a volte odia anche gli adulti, ma ciò non toglie che il suo disaccordo resti limitato alla natura: essi infatti gli sembrano 'incomprensibili' come 'bestie'
>
> (Falaschi, p. 121)[14]

What Pin hates in men is what they have in common with him and, furthermore, it is only with this type of man, in whom he recognizes himself, that he can establish a contact which transcends hatred itself. Thus the great friend turns out to be the lonely and unhappy Cugino, his sister's executioner, while the heroism of Lupo Rosso (*Romanzi e racconti* I, 37 and 48), and the cloying and religious goodness of the old people in the wood (*Romanzi e racconti* I, 140) are the very characteristics which make Pin uneasy and ultimately cause him to withdraw, as he realizes that he has nothing in common with them.

[14] G. Falaschi, *La resistenza armata nella narrativa italiana* (Turin, Einaudi, 1976), p. 121.

These episodes confirm the line of Kim's political and strategic thought: he believes in the basic positivity of banding together among like-minded men, because only among such men does one sense any real human contact, and the struggle to affirm oneself does not run counter to that of affirming others.

In this sense the fable of Pin's existential loneliness and his desire for redemption have the positive connotation needed for involvement in History, and he becomes the mascot of the partisan war. But he is a mascot who is unknowing, unaware: only for Kim 'tutto è chiaro' (*Romanzi e racconti* I, 110). As Calvino was to say in connection with the 'verità' of fairy-tales, in the preface to his editorial work of almost a decade later, when he saw that their pattern as revealing:

> la comune sorte di soggiacere ad incantesimi, cioè d'esser determinato da forze complesse e sconosciute, e lo sforzo per liberarsi e autodeterminarsi inteso come un dovere elementare, insieme a quello di liberare gli altri, anzi il non potersi liberare da soli, il liberarsi liberando
>
> (*Fiabe italiane*, p. XVIII)[15]

Pin's integrity lies in not surrendering to the possibility of some momentary salvation, either by enrolling in the black brigade, an offer made to him during his journey to prison, or by staying on in the hut in the wood with the old people. In the first case his reasoning is that he would fail to live up to his own sense of identity:

> Ma i tedeschi e i fascisti sono razze imberbi o bluastre con cui non ci si può intendere
>
> (*Romanzi e racconti* I, 29)

and in the second that he would be escaping from History:

> Ma Pin non è abituato a trattare con la gente buona e si trova a disagio, e nemmeno a dire il rosario è abituato; così mentre i due vecchi ruminano le preghiere, a occhi chiusi, lui scende dalla sua sedia piano piano e va via.
>
> (*Romanzi e racconti* I, 140)

In both cases Pin makes his choice on the basis of his own difference, of an awareness of a lack of relationship as real as the momentary convenience of the choice under offer. This is a type of self-determination in the name of integrity (a theme that we shall find again in Calvino, but never as spontaneous and unpremeditated as for the character of Pin),[16] aware though he is of his own negative aspects, those which he cannot explain to himself, and in

[15] I. Calvino, *Fiabe italiane raccolte dalla tradizione popolare durante gli ultimi cento anni e trascritte in lingua dai vari dialetti da Italo Calvino,* I and II (Turin, Einaudi, 1956), I, XVIII. Still in connection with solidarity and interdependence see 'Buon a nulla': 'E tutti gli uomini hanno un loro nodo alla scarpa, una loro cosa che non sanno fare; una loro incapacità che li lega agli altri uomini. La società si regge ormai su questa simmetria degli uomini: è un incastro di pieni e di vuoti' (*Romanzi e racconti* III, 830). This is also a historical morality of which we find a very similar expression in Merleau-Ponty's discussion on freedom: 'Ferai-je cette promesse? Risquerai-je ma vie pour si peu? Donnerai-je ma liberté pour sauver la liberté? Il n'y a pas de réponse théorique à ces questions. Mais il y a des choses qui se présentent, irrécusables, il y a cette personne aimée devant toi, il y a ces hommes qui existent esclaves autour de toi et ta liberté ne peut se voloir sans sortir de sa singularité et sans voloir la liberté.' M. Merleau-Ponty, *Phénoménologie de la perception* (Paris, Gallimard, 1942), p. 501.

[16] See again Merleau-Ponty: 'le choix véritable est celui de notre manière d'être au monde', in *Phénoménologie de la perception* (Paris, Gallimard, 1942), p. 501.

others as a dark force, the 'comune sorte di soggiacere ad incantesimi, cioè d'essere determinato da forze complesse e sconosciute' (*Fiabe italiane*, p. XVIII).

Pin's violence is directed preferably at nature, because it is upon defenceless nature that he can vent his own desire for revenge. In itself the nature which surrounds Pin cannot be called hostile: indeed, with the exception of lice and the odd bite from Babeuf, the falcon belonging to Mancino, this part of the landscape is essentially benign. But difference from himself is what triggers off Pin's destructive passion, so that toads are slimy, crickets have absurd horse-faces, spiders and fireflies are disgusting creepy-crawlies. Since animals are monstrous for him, Pin imagines that he is equally monstrous for them and he is aware of his own cruelty:

> Pin è cattivo con le bestie: sono esseri mostruosi e incomprensibili come gli uomini; dev'essere brutto essere una piccola bestia, cioè essere verde e fare la cacca a gocce, e avere sempre paura che venga un essere umano come lui, con un'enorme faccia piena d'efelidi rosse e nere e con dita capaci di fare a pezzi i grilli.
>
> (*Romanzi e racconti* I, 24)

This cruelty is presented as an act of revenge for Pin's frustrations, and his enforced loneliness leads him to tear up everything that cannot possibly fill his void by becoming the longed-for friend. Similarly, the symbolic value he attributes to the pistol implies on the one hand an ability to strike things that are far away, and make different and incongruous targets attainable and interconnectable, while on the other hand its ownership will ensure him those characteristics of power and bravery which would earn him friendship and respect. Of the two strands, the latter is undoubtedly the stronger, but it proves impracticable, just as the former is convincing only in theory; in practice it is a boring game.

Because of these frustrations he fires the pistol as a heedless gesture aimed not only at no object or animal in particular, but at the spiders' nest, a symbol of the associative life from which he feels excluded, as he feels excluded from human society:

> Pin è preso da spavento prima, e poi da gioia: tutto è stato così bello e l'odore della polvere è così buono. Ma la cosa che lo spaventa davvero è che le rane tacciono d'improvviso, e non si sente più niente come se quello sparo avesse ucciso tutta la terra.
>
> (*Romanzi e racconti* I, 25)

To kill the earth would be tantamount to losing the very hope of finding a point of contact with the world, to remaining, this time, well and truly alone.

> Poi una rana, molto distante, ricomincia a cantare, e poi un'altra più vicina, e altre più vicine ancora, finché il coro riprende e a Pin sembra gridino più forte, molto più forte di prima. E dalle case un cane abbaia e una donna si mette a chiamare dalla finestra. Pin non sparerà più perché quei silenzi e quei rumori gli fanno paura.
>
> (*Romanzi e racconti* I, 25)

Thus the world is not over, but the concerted way it starts up again frightens Pin once more, like an act of aggression rebounding upon him, to his detriment. Yet his project of revenge and punishment — against whom? his sister? society? — is merely postponed:

> Però un'altra notte tornerà e non ci sarà nulla che potrà spaventarlo e allora sparerà tutti i colpi della pistola anche contro i pipistrelli e i gatti che girano a quell'ora intorno ai pollai.
>
> (*Romanzi e racconti* I, 25)

We shall see that his brutality is related to his problematical relationship with human beings at the beginning of Chapter VIII when, from the new encampment in the wood, Pin discovers the natural world with different, less worried eyes, at least for a time. There is a direct allusion to forgetting 'le vecchie strade dove stagna l'orina dei muli' (*Romanzi e racconti* I, 88) and then to 'essere ripreso dal contagio peloso e ambiguo del carnaio umano' (*Romanzi e racconti* I, 89) with a consequent worsening of his behaviour.

It is Cugino, an ambiguously paternal figure, who teaches Pin the rudiments of respect for nature, through empathy:

> — Dai, buttaci dentro il fiammifero, — dice Pin — vediamo se esce il ragno. —
> — Perché povera bestia? — fa il Cugino — Non vedi quanti danni hanno già avuto?
> — Di', Cugino, credi che li rifaranno, i nidi? —
>
> (*Romanzi e racconti* I, 145)

The same applies to the observations on the fireflies in the concluding passage:

> — C'è pieno di lucciole —, dice il Cugino
> — A vederle da vicino, le lucciole, — dice Pin, — son bestie schifose anche loro, rossicce. —
> — Sì, — dice il Cugino, — ma viste così sono belle. —
>
> (*Romanzi e racconti* I, 147)

That Cugino, with his punitive and criminal misogyny, should constitute the most desirable model for Pin may seem questionable, but it is perfectly in line with the rest of the narrative. Perhaps this may be understood as a far broader narrative archetype: according to Dante's salvation teleology, human redemption passes first through Hell, to reach Paradise at the end of the road. The same occurs here: as the title tells us, the starting-point is *Il sentiero dei nidi di ragno*, with all the clearly negative and obscurely positive connotations referred to above. The relationship established between Pin and Cugino certainly leads them immediately to evaluate their relation with the world, to amend their own judgements, to rediscover the possibility of hope. The night-time vision: 'Il buio è punteggiato da piccoli chiarori' (*Romanzi e racconti* I, 147) seems to symbolize the dawning hope of rebirth, as slight as the light of the fireflies.

'La casa degli alveari'

The only dissonant note in this story vis-à-vis the other texts brought together in this chapter lies in the uncertainty as to its temporal setting. If we accept Lukács' observations on the basically historical nature of realism and on its ideology's faith in human fellowship, then placing this story alongside the others may seem unjustified at first sight. But it too may be considered as a realist text if we take the story as an illustration of the negative nature of human isolation and the destructiveness of fleeing from History.[17]

The story is a monologue spoken by a madman who has long rejected human society and lives in the company of bees and goats on the hillside.[18] It opens with a description of the difficulty of reaching, or even seeing, the house in which he lives:

> È difficile vederla da lontano e anche uno che c'è già stato una volta non ricorda la strada per tornarci; un sentiero c'era e l'ho distrutto a vangate, coprendolo di rovi che attecchissero e cancellassero ogni traccia. Casa mia me la son scelta bene, perduta su questa riva di ginestre, bassa a un piano che non è vista da valle, bianca per un intonaco calcinoso, ròsa dai buchi delle finestre come un osso.
>
> ('La casa degli alveari', *Romanzi e racconti* I, 217)[19]

and proceeds slowly backwards towards the description of an episode of rape and an unconvincing denial of the subsequent murder.

As the previously quoted paragraph explains, the narrator's isolation on the hills is total, yet his hatred of the human race is unremitting. In the destructive heat of the monologue, nature is evoked as a force which the narrator hopes may dispose of humanity by abolishing history:

> Al mattino girato il dorso del crinale, sotto, vedo la vallata che scende e il mare altissimo, tutt'intorno a me e al mondo. E ai piedi del mare vedo le case del genere umano pigiate, naufragate nella loro falsa fraternità, la città fulva e calcinosa, vedo il baluginare dei suoi vetri e il fumo dei suoi fuochi. Un giorno roveti ed erbe ricopriranno le sue piazze, e salirà il mare a modellare in rocce le rovine delle loro case.
>
> (*Romanzi e racconti* I, 218)

The breath of the landscape vista contemplated is proportionate to the intensity of the observer's feelings, particularly in this view which adds the spatial dimension of the pattern sea-city-hills to the temporal and apocalyptic one of the future return to a pre-human stage. But contrary to his wishes, the present bears witness rather to the destruction of the environment:

> I poveri alla domenica vengono a far legna nei boschi che si spelano come teste chiazzate d'alopecia: i tronchi trascinati con corde formano piste scoscese dove la

[17] See G. Lukàcs, *The Meaning of Contemporary Realism* (London, Merlin, 1963). In his first chapter 'The ideology of Modernism', Lukàcs convincingly contrasts the 'opposed views of the world-dynamic and developmental on the one hand [realism], static and sensational on the other [modernism]'. The former is based on the conviction that man is a social animal, the latter that he 'is by nature solitary, asocial, unable to enter into relationship with other human beings'. There is a solitude which is also part of traditional realism, but it is individual, specific to certain social or historic circumstances (Lukàcs 1963, pp. 19–20).

[18] See in this connection Falcetto's note: 'Il racconto esce per prima volta in volta nel volume nel 1949. Viene ripreso poi, senza variazioni testuali, nelle edizioni del 1969 (singolarmente collocato nella sezione di taglio autobiografico) e del 1976' (*Romanzi e racconti* I, 1284).

[19] In this connection note the affinity between this description and those of Irene (for the problem of paths running downhill), and Bauci (so high as to appear invisible) in *Le città invisibili*, now in *Romanzi e racconti* II, 423, 463–64.

> pioggia roglia nei temporali provocando frane. Così tutto rovinasse sulle città del genere umano, potessi un giorno andando vedere emergere cime di fumaioli dalla terra, incontrare gomiti di strade interrotte in mezzo a dirupi, e nel fondo di foreste radure irte di binari.
>
> (*Romanzi e racconti* I, 219)[20]

Here, comparing the condition of the wood to that of alopecia has the effect of humanizing the landscape more effectively than does the comparable simile already used in 'Uomo nei gerbidi':

> Più sotto comincia la nuvolaglia degli uliveti, più su i boschi fulvi e spelacchiati dagli incendi come schiene di vecchi cani.
>
> (*Romanzi e racconti* I, 187)

Thus in the narrator's critical view work is a form of parasitism, with the inference that human relationships conceal a sort of mutual pilfering of the spoils won. In his case, rebellion consists in denying his own need for others. He insistently stresses the pointlessness, for him, of work and exchange, because he has only himself to feed and lives on honey, snails and fruits of the forest, like an anchorite. But his behaviour is not inspired by love of nature, only by his horror of society:

> non crediate che io ami le bestie selvatiche, che sia un adoratore idillico della natura, assurde ipocrisie degli uomini.
>
> (*Romanzi e racconti* I, 218)

More explicitly than in *Il sentiero dei nidi di ragno*, both animals and families of animals are used as comparisons with human society: the more destructive and aloof they are, the more they are valued:

> E non scaccio i roveti, quelli che stanno montando sul tetto della casa e quelli che già calano sul coltivato come una valanga lenta; mi piacerebbe seppellissero tutto, me compreso. Poi ramarri han fatto il nido negli interstizi dei muri, sotto i mattoni del pavimento le formiche hanno scavato città porose e ora escono a file. Io guardo ogni giorno contento e m'accorgo d'una nuova crepa che s'apre; e penso alle città del genere umano quando soffocheranno inghiottite dalle piante selvatiche calate a valle [...] Odio i cani, quella loro servile fedeltà all'uomo, odio tutti gli animali domestici, il loro fingere di capire il genere umano per leccare gli avanzi dei suoi piatti bisunti. Solo le capre sopporto perché non dànno confidenza e non ne prendono.
>
> (*Romanzi e racconti* I, 217)

[20] Here we might note that 'potessi un giorno andando vedere' in the passage quoted follows the pattern of a line by Montale, 'Forse un mattino andando in un'aria di vetro', the opening of one of the *Ossi di seppia* which undoubtedly inspired Calvino, as he himself was to explain in the 1976 text entitled 'Eugenio Montale, *Forse un mattino andando*' in *Saggi* II, 1179–89. Note also the influence of this poem on 'Il lampo' (1943); *Romanzi e racconti* III, 777–78, and also on 'Dietro il retrovisore'; *Romanzi e racconti* III, 1159–63 forty years later. See also G. Bertone, *Italo Calvino: Il castello della scrittura* (Turin, Einaudi, 1994), p. 246.

Whereas what Pin hates about animals is what most distances them from humanity, this narrator hates what brings them closest. The only real exception is bees:

> Solo le api, sono con me, ora: brulicano intorno alle mie mani senza pungermi quando tolgo il miele dalle arnie, e mi si posano addosso come una barba vivente, amiche api, dalla ragione antica e senza storia.
>
> (*Romanzi e racconti* I, 218)

This would seem the only kind of contact enjoyed by this hapless narrator were it not for his reference to reading:

> Ma ogni notte, quando le colline sono perdute nel buio e io non riesco a seguire il ragionamento d'un vecchio libro al lume della lanterna, e la città del genere umano con le sue luci e le sue musiche è giù in fondo, io sento le voci di voi tutti che m'accusate.
>
> (*Romanzi e racconti* I, 220)

However indirect, the message of any text presupposes some contact between a transmitter and a recipient, so that we may consider the reference to reading as a direct contradiction of the narrator's claims to total isolation and sense an element of inconsistency. Yet if this were the case, it would be hard to explain how this story could have survived various revisions to retain this form, given Calvino's well-known vigilance and propensity for detailed rewriting.

It is more probable, therefore that this reference provides not so much the key to the whole monologue, as the answer to the complications aroused by its being placed in the autobiographical section of *I racconti*. If we see the figure of this guilty anchorite in association with those of the various portraits of uncommitted readers such as Zena il Lungo in *Il sentiero dei nidi di ragno* and Gian dei Brughi in *Il barone rampante*, ultimately condemned by the working out of the plot, it is understandable that it should be the narrator himself who declares his sense of guilt, given that what we have here is a monologue. In this case literary interests are pursued at the expense of landed property, along the lines of the already mentioned authorial 'rimorso di aver lasciato la campagna in mano ai fittavoli' (*Saggi* II, 2730). Just as the apocalyptic tone and reference to a diet of honey and snails — always making allowances for the divergences represented by both the religious aspect of the discourse and the diet, which in his case consisted of wild honey and locusts - are reminiscent of John the Baptist (Matthew 3, 4) and seem once again to suggest San Giovanni, the name of the author's family holding.

This does not explain the rape and murder of the 'donna nera della falce' (*Romanzi e racconti* I, 220), an obvious image of death, but the symbol of a remorse which is the reverse of obvious, particularly if it is to be interpreted as a deliberately autobiographical feature. But if we can consider the narrator as a guilty projection of the author, then we might regard the woman as embodying a murder which is not real, but literary. We might note that the narrator makes three references to the 'strisce di prato' above his house where the body of the woman is buried: the same expression is used twice in *Il sentiero dei nidi di ragno* to indicate the place where the spies are buried. We might also note that the narrator denies having committed the crime and maintains that no one can accuse him because no one can have seen him, just as Cugino's killing of la Nera in *Il sentiero dei nidi di ragno* cannot be proved, since it is not explicit in the text. Lastly, the woman in 'La casa degli alveari' is described as black, and Pin's sister is called Nera.[21]

Even if we consider it convincing, this interpretation is nonetheless incomplete: if we try to square it with the autobiographical framework, the relationship between narrator and bees remains far from clear, just as we do not understand what bees, honey and hives are meant to represent on this level. Traditionally, honey would suggest the sweetness of poetry, but then the bees, those 'amiche api, dalla ragione antica e senza storia', would become poets, a transformation which is not convincing in its denial of history.[22]

What seems clear is the explicit link between isolation and sense of guilt. On an autobiographical level it also seems probable that both on the basis of the isolation which creativity entails, and understood as remorse for a past lack of self-control, the sense of guilt might once again provide the link between subject and landscape.

L'entrata in guerra

Still within the sphere of realistic landscape representation, we now move to a trio of stories ('L'entrata in guerra', 'Gli avanguardisti a Mentone', 'Le notti dell'UNPA') published together under the title of the first named.[23]

Together, they represent the clearest attempt Calvino ever made to immerse himself in his own memory in order to reproduce the past and to search in it for the roots of his own actions. Overtly autobiographical in character (see p. 72 below), the central episodes are put forward to serve as examples, that is, in such a way as to cast light upon the state of mind of the very young Calvino in connection with the war and the fascist rhetoric which generated it.

That individual point of view which the narrator had decided not to emphasize at the time of *Il sentiero dei nidi di ragno* is now reconstructed, years later, without awkwardness of any kind. The untroubled, confident and mature voice of the narrator questions and portrays the adolescent he once was, analyses his behaviour and attitudes, breaks down his

21 Calvino's unease vis-à-vis his first book is well documented by the introduction to his first, late reissue, see *Nota introduttiva 1954* in *Romanzi e racconti* I, 1205–07. See F. Pedriali, 'Più per paura che per gioco?: Three Textual Explorations of Calvino's *Il sentiero*', in *MLR*, 93, 1, 1998, pp. 59–70. According to Falcetto, further proof of the author's attempt to curb the misogyny of the text is provided by the subsequent reissues of Calvino which progressively toned down at least the most obvious and offensive examples, see *Romanzi e racconti* I, 1248–49. For an exemplary analysis of the broader misogyny in the text see C. Milanini, *L'utopia discontinua: saggio su Italo Calvino* (Milan, Garzanti, 1990), pp. 30–34.

22 Martin McLaughlin reached similar, if not identical conclusions in his paper read to the Symposium on Calvino held at the University of Warwick in 1988. It was part of the analysis of the pronounced anti-intellectual thought of the young Calvino, documented in M. McLaughlin, 'Calvino's Library: Labyrinth or Laboratory?', in *Italian Storytellers: Essays on Narrative Literature*, edited by E. Haywood and C. O'Cuilleanain (Dublin, Irish Academic Press, 1989).

23 The useful information about the text by Mario Barenghi includes an unpublished typescript by the author and a number of variants which the author expunged from all editions subsequent the one in 1954; see *Romanzi e racconti* I, 1316–28. The most relevant for this study is the cutting out of two references to the Casinò; for their insertion would have made the identification of the place much easier, given the small number of Casinò in Italy.

models of behaviour, to the point of recognizing, in what I see as an affectionate and elegiac tone, his debt to the old-style bourgeois values, inculcated in him by the family circle, and the reason for innate opposition to the regime, in clear contrast to the arrogance of the new fascist rhetoric.

Furthermore, it should also be noted that these particular stories are very untypical of Calvino: the weight of truth lies a little too heavily upon the figure of the adolescent, whose main feature is an austere reticence, a moralism masked by irony which makes him embarrassed, unforthcoming, isolated from his friends. Calvino, so skilled at representing adolescents from the outside, is a little less incisive with this internalized and realistic viewpoint: not wanting to attribute to his former self other virtues than those of having been able to keep faith with the family grounding of honesty and respect for work and nature in which he had grown up, the narrator seems almost to want to keep to a paradigmatic view of an adolescent from a respectable family, and the narrative is somewhat impersonal as a result.[24]

Set in Sanremo in the summer of 1940, all three stories begin with the description of an adolescent on holiday, rather bored but also free at last to spend the day as he chooses. From one story to the next we are given the sense of a gradual maturing, in a noticeable growth of confidence:

> Erano tempi che non avevamo voglia di niente.
>
> (*Romanzi e racconti* I, 485)

> Dopo cena non vedevo l'ora di uscire a passeggio benché quasi non facessi altro tutto il giorno. Forse proprio in quel tempo venivo prendendo gusto a vivere [...] Così conoscevo il pessimismo e l'esaltazione dei tempi, e confusamente vivevo, e andavo a spasso.
>
> (*Romanzi e racconti* I, 499)

> Ero un ragazzo tardo; a sedici anni per l'età che avevo ero piuttosto indietro in molte cose. Poi, improvvisamente nell'estate del '40, scrissi una commedia in tre atti, ebbi un amore, imparai ad andare in bicicletta.
>
> (*Romanzi e racconti* I, 525)

It seems possible that the critics who have talked of alienation in connection with these stories (see, for example, Ricci 1986, p. 31)[25] have not understood the precise implications

[24] Calvino may have been thinking of this text in 'Autobiografia politica giovanile' when he wrote: 'Ora però devo guardarmi da un altro errore o vezzo di chi scrive ricordi autobiografici; quello di tendere a configurare la propria esperienza come un'esperienza "media" di una data generazione e ambiente, mettendo in risalto gli aspetti più comuni e lasciando in ombra quelli più particolari e personali' (*Saggi* II, 2735). Another possible criticism might be the one which the author himself voiced in an interview in 1959 with Roberto de Monticelli: 'L'atteggiamento dominante nella letteratura italian più recente potrebbe essere definito come "neo-flaubertiano". La società è rappresentata con fotografica obiettività cogliendone con acume aspetti vacui e goffi e colpevoli, nei discorsi, nelle psicologie, nel "costume". Il punto di vista è quello dell'intellettuale, che guarda con ironia e distacco quella eterna commedia dell'Italia provinciale, ma può permettersi anche qualche sfumatura d'indulgenza, di compatimento, di nostalgia. Quest'atteggiamento che anch'io ho sparsamente praticato non mi soddisfa. Porta a una descrittività statica, passiva e stanca. Ed è stato ormai divulgato, nella sua versione giornalistica, dai rotocalchi intellettuali' (*Saggi* II, 2722).

[25] F. Ricci, 'The Recovery of Mnemonic Meaning in *L'entrata in guerra*', *The Review of Contemporary Fiction*, 63/4 (Winter 1986), 31–37 (p. 31).

of Calvino's decision to highlight moments of conflict rather than moments of exaltation ('Le memorie difficili' is in fact the title with which they appeared in the 1958 edition of *I racconti*).

In the terms which most concern us here, that is, in connection with landscape, we may note that the action shifts from the sea, and some final adolescent games, to a survey of the townscape, in particular that of the 'Città Vecchia' and, finally, to an imaginary walk over the hills in the footsteps of the narrator's father.

The first story opens under a cloudy sky on the day war is declared. In the morning there are still glimpses of sunshine during which the protagonist and two other boys on a raft express their hopes that war will not be declared after all. But even those first days of June, with their uncertain weather, imply a feeling of foreboding of an early end to the holidays:

> Ai bagni quasi tutti gli ombrelloni erano chiusi;
>
> (*Romanzi e racconti* I, 485)

and the town soon becomes a crossing-point for military convoys going towards the front and tourists leaving a region regarded as a danger zone:

> Verso la stazione passava una fila di soldati. Qualcuno dalla balaustra della passeggiata applaudì. Nessuno dei soldati levò il capo.
>
> (*Romanzi e racconti* I, 486)

> Ogni tanto un treno con cannoni e truppe manovrava e ripartiva verso il confine.
>
> (*Romanzi e racconti* I, 486)

> La città era attraversata di continuo da macchine militari che andavano al fronte, e macchine borghesi che sfollavano con le masserizie legate sopra il tetto.
>
> (*Romanzi e racconti* I, 488)

> Passavano macchine militari, verso monte, verso le strade d'arroccamento alla frontiera.
>
> (*Romanzi e racconti* I, 497–98)

The theme of general movement is used to highlight the central episode of the evacuation from the frontier areas of the refugees, with whom the protagonist finds himself in contact, discovering the obverse of the way in which he had judged the war:

> Io pensavo al nostro distacco verso le cose della guerra, che con Ostero eravamo riusciti a portare a un'estrema finitezza di stile, fino a farcene una seconda natura, una corazza. Ora la guerra mi si rivelava nel portare al gabinetto i paralitici, ecco fin dove lontano mi ero spinto, ecco quante mai cose accadevano sulla terra, Ostero, che non supponeva la nostra tranquilla anglofilia.
>
> (*Romanzi e racconti* I, 496)

The speed with which soldiers and civilians are moved about — as well as the reason why Ostero does not go with the protagonist to help the refugees, namely, because his family are trying out a car to replace the one requisitioned by the army (*Romanzi e racconti* I, 489) — contrasts with the slowness of the evacuees and the discomforts of their journey:

> Salii per la gradinata e dovevo andar piano perché avanti a me sostenevano una vecchia
>
> (*Romanzi e racconti* I, 490)

At all events, there is already a divergence between the general town dwellers' neurosis, as they invent spy stories in the usual search for a scapegoat (*Romanzi e racconti* I, 487) and the thinking of the boy's family circle, with his mother refusing to give in to the false rhetoric of this second world war as compared with the memory she had of the first, and his father who:

> ora vedeva anche sconvolgersi lo scenario immutabile delle montagne familiari a lui dall'infanzia,
>
> (*Romanzi e racconti* I, 488)

with a deeply-felt concern both for the hardships of human beings and for the adverse effect upon agriculture and nature in general.

> Ora vedeva le fasce abbandonate tornar gerbide, i muri a secco franare, e dai boschi emigrare, spaventate dai colpi di cannone le ultime famiglie di cinghiali che ogni autunno egli inseguiva con i suoi cani
>
> (*Romanzi e racconti* I, 488)

For the protagonist, help for the refugees is a source of greater discomfort, the resurfacing of a sense of injustice which has made him middle-class, and has made them dispossessed.

> perché loro, questa gente, per me erano già stati una pena, un rimprovero — per me diverso da mio padre — a vederli, che so? Imbastare dei muli, aprire all'acqua i solchi di una vigna con la vanga, senza poter con loro mai avere un rapporto, mai pensare di venir loro in aiuto.
>
> (*Romanzi e racconti* I, 490)

In the face of such wretchedness a single, bitter certainty comes to the mind of the boy in the uniform of an *avanguardista*:

> Io tutta questa gente non l'amavo.
>
> (*Romanzi e racconti* I, 490)

Then comes another horrible discovery, utterly personal this time, which, as Germana Pescio Bottino rightly points out,[26] foreshadows the passage 'Era un'Italia nascosta...' in

[26] See G. Pescio-Bottino, *Calvino* (Florence, La nuova Italia, 1976), p. 31, and also G. C. Ferretti, *Le capre di Bikini: Calvino giornalista e saggista 1945–1985* (Rome, Editori Riuniti, 1989), pp. 92–94. Between 'L'entrata in guerra' and *La giornata di uno scrutatore* there are remarkable similarities. Both narratives portray historical events realistically and the dramatic or even tragic quality of the times is shown through the suffering brought about for those beings who are not even responsible for their own actions. Calvino's ethical stance seems to be the magnetic field generated by the opposite poles of 'insensatezza colpevole' and 'alterità innocente'; G. C. Ferretti, *Le capre di Bikini: Calvino giornalista e saggista 1945–1985* (Rome, Editori Riuniti, 1989), p. 148. For an interesting analysis of the ethical implications in Calvino see also A. Berardinelli, 'Calvino moralista: ovvero, restare sani dopo la fine del mondo', *Diario*, 9 (February 1991), pp. 37–58 and C. Milanini, *L'utopia discontinua: saggio su Italo Calvino* (Milan, Garzanti, 1990), pp. 164–67 and pp. 184–87.

La giornata di uno scrutatore (*Romanzi e racconti* II, 20) — that of the faces of some of the evacuees, disfigured by mental, or hereditary, illness:

> era questo volto buio dei paesi montanari ora obbligato a svelarsi, a sfilare in parata il vecchio segreto delle famiglie contadine attorno a cui le case dei paesi si stringono una all'altra come le scaglie di una pigna.
>
> (*Romanzi e racconti* I, 493)

The *avanguardista*, now without his uniform, ends up by mingling with this slow, macabre, war-induced procession, in the grim paradox in which the federal inspector mistakes him for a relative of the dead paralytic old man, and shakes his hand in condolence.

This painful episode has at least clarified matters: the war, which at the beginning of the story had appeared as an obstacle to the holidays, an irritation, has now become a certainty; the return home, as for a soldier on leave, has become a short-lived illusion for the protagonist too.

> Era una sera chiara, il cielo era rossiccio, io salivo una via tra case e pergole.
>
> (*Romanzi e racconti* I, 497)

A temporary lull, but one which will not be shattered by the excitement of the moment:

> A un tratto ci fu un muoversi, un correre sul marciapiede, un impigliarsi di tende cacciamosca alle botteghe di frutta e di barbiere, e dicevano: — Sì, sì è lui, guarda lì, è il duce, è il duce.
>
> (*Romanzi e racconti* I, 498)

An epilogue to a novella of movement is provided by the passing of Mussolini's open car, the theatricality of his gesture and above all the detachment with which the narrator already views Mussolini as more immature than himself.

> La mia città, interrotto per la guerra il suo turismo, si era come rappresa nella sua scorza provinciale; io la sentivo più familiare e più misurabile.
>
> (*Romanzi e racconti* I, 499)

These are the narrator's reflections at the beginning of this second story, where the main theme is the interface between private and public space, so that the open air seems precisely to put the stress upon the protagonist's walk through the town in search of his friend Biancone.

> Nei soliti bigliardi non c'era; per andare a casa sua bisognava salire per la città vecchia. Sotto i neri archivolti le lampade imbrattate d'azzurro mandavano una luce falsa che non raggiungeva i margini dei vicoli e delle rampe acciottolate, ma si rifletteva solo sulle strisce di pittura bianca che segnavano i gradini; e indovinavo di passare accanto a persone sedute al buio fuori degli usci, sulle soglie o a cavalcioni di sedie impagliate. L'ombra era come vellutata di queste presenze umane che si manifestavano in chiacchierii, improvvisi richiami e risa, sempre con un frusciante tono d'intimità: e talora nel biancheggiare di un braccio di donna o di una veste.
>
> (*Romanzi e racconti* I, 500–01)

The darkness in which the old city is plunged and in which the human presence of its inhabitants is felt, however indistinctly, contrasts with Menton, empty and abandoned:

> Ero già triste. Il lento battere del mare contro gli scogli si congiungeva al silenzio naturale della campagna e chiudevano in un cerchio la città vuota, il suo silenzio innaturale, rotto ogni tanto da rumori isolati ed eccheggianti: un solfeggio di tromba, un canto, il rombo di una moto.
>
> (*Romanzi e racconti* I, 509)

The reconstruction of these contrasting city models contains reflections on the nature of the town, and they should be seen in relation to the stories of Marco Polo in *Le città invisibili*. But for the moment we are concerned more with the link between the following passage and *Il sentiero dei nidi di ragno*:

> Dal buio di un'arcata sbucai alla fine sotto il cielo aperto, che solo allora vidi senza stelle ma chiaro tra le foglie d'un enorme carrubo. La città lì finiva l'aggrumo delle case e cominciava a seminarsi nella campagna, ad allungare le disordinate propaggini su per le vallate. Oltre il muro d'un orto le ombre bianche delle ville sul versante opposto filtravano solo esigui spiragli di luce intorno ai telai delle finestre. Una strada fiancheggiata, da una rete metallica scendeva a mezza costa verso il torrente, e là in una casetta sormontata da un terrazzo a pergola abitava Biancone. Mi avvicinai nell'aria quieta e sussurrante di canne e fischiai verso la casa.
>
> (*Romanzi e racconti* I, 501)

This is probably Pin's favourite area, but it is described in *Il sentiero dei nidi di ragno* so as to achieve completely different effects:

> È notte. Pin ha scantonato fuori dal mucchio delle vecchie case, per le stradine che vanno tra orti e scoscendimenti ingombri d'immondizie. Nel buio le reti metalliche che cintano i semenzai gettano una maglia d'ombre sulla terra grigio lunare [...] [il posto delle tane dei ragni] è una scorciatoia sassosa che scende al torrente tra le due pareti di terra e d'erba.
>
> (*Romanzi e racconti* I, 23)

In both there is the transition between the enclosed space and the expanse of countryside: in 'Gli avanguardisti a Mentone' the human presence is sought in the lights filtering from distant windows, a desire for order and quiet as a contrast to the round-ups soon to be disclosed, whereas in *Il sentiero dei nidi di ragno* the stress is on the disorderly, the ghostly, the sense of human absence, which are more in keeping with Pin's fear and loneliness. This same area recurs as the opening setting for the third and most successful of these stories. Once again it is the meeting place between the young Calvino and his friend Biancone, between the diffidence of the one and the playfulness of the other. Together the two boys begin to explore the night, making it the backdrop for jokes and adventures, but Calvino remains slightly aloof, with a lingering moralism which distances him from the arrogance of his friend, which he finds false and exaggerated. Two presences now take shape in the sleeping town, the presence of those who work during the day, and the hedonistic and ugly presence of the frequenters of gaming dens and brothels. Instinctively both boys side with the former;

as a squad of militia passes by singing a rowdy song, almost as though in contempt of that hard-earned sleep, the character feels a sudden prophetic awareness:

> L'irruzione loro in quel punto portò un vento di violenza; mi s'aggricciò la pelle come a un tratto fossi piombato nella guerra civile, una guerra il cui fuoco era da sempre durato nella cenere e di tanto in tanto levava una lingua di fuoco.
>
> (*Romanzi e racconti* I, 538)

The adventures which follow take place within the dark space of the 'Città Vecchia': they include the sighting of a Communist, the advances of a greasy pimp, a visit to a horse-faced prostitute (once again like la Nera di Carrugio Lungo in *Il sentiero dei nidi di ragno*) and to a brothel, until the two characters part, the young protagonist going off, disappointed, to look at the sea, though it holds no attraction for him. He watches the departure of the fishermen who have to be out at sea by dawn, and he feels the contradiction, the conflict between that peaceful, hard-working world and the world of the false bragging of the night-walkers more strongly than ever.

Later, at dawn, the two boys finally decide to go to bed, but the protagonist cannot sleep: he imagines his father, already up and walking around his estate:

> E forse i soli momenti suoi felici erano questi dell'alba, quando passava col suo cane per le note strade, liberando i bronchi dal catarro che l'opprimeva la notte e guardando pian piano dal grigio indistinto nascere i colori nei filari di vigne, tra i rami degli olivi, e riconoscendo il fischio degli uccelli mattinieri uno per uno.
>
> (*Romanzi e racconti* I, 545)[27]

This identification with the father figure implies the conscious espousal of the values for which his father is the mouthpiece, but also a return to those rows of vine, that dawn of colour, dictated by the aesthetic choice of a privileged place, rich in emotional memories.

[27] Cristina Benussi comments most convincingly on the link between the writing of *L'entrata in guerra* and the death of Mario Calvino, the author's father: '[Questi racconti] Scritti nel 1953 dopo la morte del padre avvenuta il 25 ottobre 1951, dopo un evento che di solito scatena il desiderio di ricordare [...] È questo l'unico libro in cui il calore della famiglia fa da contrappunto al freddo della storia; per questo mi sembra di poterlo ritenere quasi un omaggio alla memoria, più che storica, come voleva la collana cui era destinato, familiare, dal momento che dai suoi, prima che da qualsiasi altro libro o esperienza, aveva imparato a essere contro ad ogni fascismo', C. Benussi, *Introduzione a Italo Calvino* (Bari, Laterza, 1989), pp. 33–36.

CHAPTER II

The Landscape of the Fairy-Tale

The only one of the 'fairy-tale' works by Calvino to include a landscape which completely and recognizably reintroduces the sea–city–hills pattern of the Sanremo countryside is *Il visconte dimezzato.*

In 'La tradizione popolare nelle fiabe' (1973) we read that although studies on the narrative scheme of fairy-tales have revealed how much versions told in very different countries and completely different historical/social conditions have in common, the fairy-tale does contain indications which enable it to be localized in both time and place and that:

> ridurre la fiaba al suo scheletro invariante contribuisce a mettere in evidenza quante variabili geografiche e storiche formano il rivestimento di questo scheletro. [...] La fiaba, nella formalizzazione di Propp, non può prendere le mosse se non da una funzione di *danneggiamento* o *mancanza*, e non è un caso che, esaminando le raccolte dei folkloristi, il massimo di specificità temporale e locale si noti appunto nelle sequenze iniziali, nelle avversità della situazione di partenza, mentre lo sviluppo e la soluzione fortunata sono più spesso stereotipe e lontane dall'esperienza vissuta del narrante e del suo pubblico (le solite nozze con il solito principe o la solita principessa).
>
> (*Saggi* II, 1615–16)

At first sight, the beginning of *Il visconte dimezzato* where the setting is made explicit and, indeed, Bohemia is actually mentioned seems to form an exception to these observations on the popular fairy-tale:

> C'era una guerra contro i turchi. Il visconte Medardo di Terralba, mio zio, cavalcava per la pianura di Bohemia diretto all'accampamento dei cristiani.
>
> (*Romanzi e racconti* I, 367)

And, indeed, we can explain the discrepancy only by considering *Il visconte dimezzato* as a narrative which uses the scheme of the popular fairy-tale, but which is in fact the original creation of an author and not part of an oral tradition. From 'Nota 1960' ('Postfazione ai *Nostri antenati*', *Romanzi e racconti* I, 1208–19) we learn that the author's prime concern was to move away from a tradition, rather than conforming to one as an oral narrator would probably have done:

> Dunque, da un po' di tempo pensavo a un uomo tagliato in due per lungo, e che ognuna delle due parti andava per conto suo. La storia di un soldato, in una guerra

> moderna? Ma la solita satira espressionista era fritta e rifritta: meglio una guerra dei tempi andati, i Turchi, un colpo di scimitarra, no: meglio un colpo di cannone, così si sarebbe creduto che una metà era andata distrutta, invece poi saltava fuori. Allora i Turchi col cannone? Sì, le guerre austro-turche, fine Seicento, ma tutto lasciato un po' nel vago, il romanzo storico non m'interessava (ancora).
>
> (*Romanzi e racconti* I, 1210)

What has to be inferred in a fairy-tale in the popular tradition, through a laborious network of suppositions, is revealed in an original work by the date of composition and, if one is luckier still, by introductory notes. Thus we discover without much effort that the war against the Turks stands for the Second World War and the cleaving in two of Medardo represents the tensions of the subsequent cold war. But it is interesting to note that the historical setting of *Il visconte dimezzato* serves to mask in a more distant and veiled fashion conflicts which are nearer in time. We know that the war is occurring in Bohemia because we are told as much explicitly, which is rarely the case in fairy stories: indeed the function of 'absence' (or 'lack') and 'injury' (Propp 1928, pp. 25–65)[1] (articulated here at two distinct moments of the narrative, as we shall see) also serves to create that aura of wonder which tells the reader that this is indeed a fairy-tale.

The Bohemian plain offers no particularly 'Bohemian' characteristics to the eyes of the future lieutenant Medardo. We know that he has left behind him 'l'ultimo castello in mano cristiana' (*Romanzi e racconti* I, 367); there is talk of a barren plain, of countryside shrivelled by drought, of dried-up rivers, of stubble and bushes: in short of a desolate, but indeterminate landscape. What gives the panorama specificity and at the same time alerts the reader to the fairy-tale nature of the situation, are the visual incongruities and the grotesque (and fantastical) explanations of the groom Curzio.

Thus it can be argued that the first chapter is devoted to performing the function of absence: absence of normality in the general situation (storks, flamingoes and cranes in place of eagles, piles of human corpses at first sight inexplicably feathered, etc.) and a symmetrical absence of normality in the non-existent reactions of the protagonist:

> In cuore non aveva né nostalgia, né dubbio, né apprensione. [...] Sentiva il sangue di quella guerra crudele, sparso per mille rivi sulla terra, giungere fino a lui; e se ne lasciava lambire, senza provare accanimento né pietà.
>
> (*Romanzi e racconti* I, 371)

'Injury' appears, in the form of a cannon-ball, in the second chapter, at the end of which the vicissitudes of the half-hero can begin. Once again we may usefully turn to 'Nota 1960' where Calvino warns the reader not to take what might seem a Manichean division into Il Buono and Il Gramo too seriously:

> Dunque: una metà sopravvive, l'altra comparirà in un secondo tempo. Come differenziarle? Il sistema d'effetto sicuro è fare una metà buona e una cattiva, un contrasto alla R. L. Stevenson, come *Dr Jeckyll and Mr Hyde* e i due fratelli del *Master of Ballantrae.* Così la storia s'organizzava su se stessa secondo uno schema

1 V. Propp, *Morphology of the Folktale* (1928). Quoted from Lawrence Scott's English translation, ninth edition (Austin, University of Texas Press, 1986), pp. 25–65.

> perfettamente geometrico. E i critici potevano cominciare ad andare su una falsa strada: dicendo che quel che mi stava a cuore era il problema del bene e del male. No, non mi stava a cuore per niente, non avevo pensato neanche per un minuto al bene e al male. Come un pittore può usare un ovvio contrasto di colori perché gli serve a dare evidenza a una forma, così io avevo usato un ben noto contrasto narrativo per dare evidenza a quel che m'interessava, cioè il dimidiamento.
>
> (*Romanzi e racconti* I, 1210–11)

The cleaving of the character is undoubtedly an event belonging to the sphere of the marvellous, and yet the cleaving of Medardo has antecedents in the literary rather than the popular fairy-tale: here, though numerous cases of bodily mutilation come to mind, they are worked by enchantment and not by almost believable agents (in this case, the cannon-ball).

Calvino explains the cleaving of Medardo in terms of the existential condition of contemporary man. As Lavagetto has elegantly and appositely observed (Lavagetto 1988, p. IX),[2] the most convincing literary antecedent for the cleaving of Medardo is to be found in the comic, prophetic and threatening argument put forward by the character of Aristophanes in the *Symposium*; though one should also bear in mind Dante's Mahomet, with his cloven trunk, among the other 'seminator[i] di scandalo e di scisma' (*Inferno* XXVIII, 22–42),[3] where 'scisma' implies an allusion to both the civil war (in other words, a fratricidal war, with important consequences for our later discussion) in Italy, and to the global cold war.

We do not find cleavings of this kind in the popular fairy-tale. However, we might also bear in mind other closely associated models of splitting, for instance the stories in which the protagonists are two brothers (more rarely sisters). This comparison is useful here because, in part, *Il visconte dimezzato* makes use of this scheme. The one briefly outlined by Bettelheim illustrates this concept:

> in other fairy tales in which two protagonists — usually brothers — stand for seemingly incompatible aspects of the human personality, the two usually separate after an original period of having been united, and then have different fates. In these fairy tales — which, though little noticed today, are among the oldest and most widely disseminated ones — the stay-at-home brother and the adventurous one remain in touch through magic. When the adventurous brother perishes because he has permitted himself to live in accordance with his desires or to disregard dangers, his brother sets out to rescue him, succeeds and forever after the two live happily reunited. The details vary [...] What all these stories have in common are features that suggest the identity of the two heroes, one of whom is cautious and reasonable, but ready to risk his life to rescue the other brother, who foolishly exposes himself to some terrible perils; and also some magic object, a life token, which usually disintegrates as soon as one dies, serving as the sign for the other to set out on the rescue.
>
> (Bettelheim 1975, pp. 90–91)[4]

[2] M. Lavagetto, preface to Italo Calvino, *Sulla fiaba* (Turin, Einaudi, 1988), pp. VII–XXVII (p. IX).

[3] *Inferno* XXVIII, 22–42.

[4] B. Bettelheim, *The Uses of Enchantment*, 1975 (London, Penguin 1978), pp. 90–91.

It is clear that in *Il visconte dimezzato* both parts of Medardo are particularly averse to the idea of a reunion, and that no magic object in the literal sense reunites them. But one might extend the category so as to include Pamela, who is after all the only character in the text to have quasi-magical powers in that she at least 'sapeva parlare alle sue bestie' (*Romanzi e racconti* I, 409). (Even the wet nurse Sebastiana, who at a certain point acts as a 'magical assistant' through her knowledge of the 'virtù di tutte le erbe', does not have supernatural powers, but owes her knowledge to her pirate father and hermit grandfather, see *Romanzi e racconti* I, 413). The two Medardos are kept in contact not exactly by magic, but by an unexplainable form of telepathy, as one deduces from il Gramo's question to Trelawney, 'Mi spieghi lei dottore ho un senso come se la gamba che non ho fosse stanca per un gran camminare. Cosa può essere questo?' (*Romanzi e racconti* I, 410), which foreshadows the return of il Buono. Furthermore, when il Gramo is nearly massacred by his fellow-countrymen for his misdeeds, he is saved by il Buono who persuades the rebels to pardon him and sends him the phial of unguent given him by the Bohemian hermits to soothe the pain of his wound (*Romanzi e racconti* I, 433).

Amongst the variants to the pattern mentioned, a very common one which Bettelheim also considered particularly significant, concerns leaving home, a step not always taken by the adventurous brother. In Grimm's tale 'The Two Brothers', both boys are originally driven from home together and divide only subsequently, taking paths which fork in the middle of the forest. Bettelheim explains:

> The forest, where they go to decide that they want to have a life of their own, symbolizes the place in which inner darkness is confronted and worked through; where uncertainty is resolved about who one is, and where one begins to understand who one wants to be.
>
> (Bettelheim 1975, p. 93)

Perhaps Calvino's decision to represent an involuntary and traumatic separation on an open battle-field may conversely be interpreted as injury taking a reluctant and psychologically unprepared character by surprise. To quote Bettelheim again:

> In the stories of the 'Two Brothers' type, the heroes are depicted as being in what we would call the adolescent age — that period in life when the relative emotional tranquillity of prepubertal child is replaced by adolescent stress and turmoil, brought about by new psychological developments. Hearing such a story, the child comprehends (at least subconsciously) that although what he is told about are adolescent conflicts, the problems are typical of our predicament whenever we are confronted with having to move from one developmental stage to the next.
>
> (Bettelheim 1975, p. 93)

These observations may help prepare the ground for the entrance of the character-narrator, Medardo's anonymous nephew. At the end of the story, after the happy fairy-tale ending, he says:

> Io invece, in mezzo a tanto fervore d'interezza, mi sentivo sempre più triste e manchevole. Alle volte uno si crede incompleto ed è soltanto giovane.

> Ero giunto sulle soglie dell'adolescenza e ancora mi nascondevo tra le radici dei grandi alberi del bosco a raccontarmi storie. Un ago di pino poteva rappresentare per me un cavaliere, o una dama, o un buffone; io lo facevo muovere dinanzi ai miei occhi e m'esaltavo in racconti interminabili. Poi mi prendeva vergogna di queste fantasticherie e scappavo.
>
> (*Romanzi e racconti* I, 444)

On this occasion, Calvino's adolescent behaves in the wood in a way very similar to the child listener analysed by Bettelheim.[5] I have quoted this passage to pinpoint the shades of ambiguity it casts on the story just told, whose truth it allows us to doubt, but also to examine more closely the place where these adolescent fantasies occur: a wood, from which one can see a town overlooking a bay; in a word, the countryside around Sanremo. From the bay we move away to the final exchanges. Trelawney, the young narrator's adult friend, acts as Medardo's benefactor, in that he is the doctor who sews the two halves together again. But before being a benefactor, Trelawney was depicted as a bungling scientist, a chaser after will-o'-the-wisps. If the point of the story is the phase of transition from adolescence to maturity, Trelawney's departure represents a farewell to the will-o'-the-wisps of childhood, which the narrator tries to pursue one last time:

> — Dottore! Dottor Trelawney! mi prenda con sé! Non può lasciarmi qui, dottore! —
>
> Ma già le navi stavano scomparendo all'orizzonte e io rimasi qui, in questo nostro mondo pieno di responsabilità e di fuochi fatui.
>
> (*Romanzi e racconti* I, 444)

'Responsibility' seems to be the keyword, all the more so in that what little previous biographical history Calvino provides for the narrator allows us to see him as a fully paid-up escapist/nature-loving daydreamer:

> Io ero libero come l'aria perché non avevo genitori e non appartenevo alla categoria dei servi né a quella dei padroni. Facevo parte della famiglia dei Terralba solo per tardivo riconoscimento, ma non portavo il loro nome e nessuno era tenuto a educarmi. La mia povera madre era figlia del visconte Aiolfo e sorella maggiore di Medardo, ma aveva macchiato l'onore della famiglia fuggendo con un bracconiere che fu poi mio padre. Io ero nato nella capanna del

[5] At all events the persistence of the state of lack at the end of the story is part of the tradition of Italian fairy-tales, which conventionally end with pairs of lines or quatrains such as: 'Fecero tanto lusso e spatusso | Ma io ero dietro l'uscio, | Per mangiare andai all'osteria | E così finisce la storia mia' (*Fiabe italiane*, p. 47); 'E tutti sono stati allegri e contenti | E a me che ero a vedere non m'hanno dato niente' (*Fiabe italiane*, p. 50); 'Con gran lusso e spatusso | E a me mi lasciarono dietro l'uscio' (*Fiabe italiane*, p. 72); 'Vissero in pace e in carità | E a me mai nessuno niente dà' (*Fiabe italiane*, p. 166); 'Così stettero e godettero | Ed a me nulla mi dettero' (*Fiabe italiane*, p. 261 and, with small variation, p. 358); 'E lì se ne stiedero, e se godiedero, | E a me nulla mi diedero. | No, mi diedero un un centesimino | E lo misi in un buchino' (*Fiabe italiane*, p. 360); 'Così vissero e godettero, | Sempre in pace se ne stettero, | Ed a me nulla mi dettero' (*Fiabe italiane*, p. 365); 'e se ne stettero contenti e consolati, mentre noi siamo rimasti qui assetati' (*Fiabe italiane*, p. 511); 'Fecero tante feste, balli, canti | E noi restammo con le mani vacanti' (*Fiabe italiane*, p. 571); 'Loro restarono felici e contenti | E noi siam qui che ci freghiamo i denti' (*Fiabe italiane*, p. 610 and, with small variation, pp. 628, 632, 668, 755); 'Loro restarono felici e contenti, | E noialtri restammo senza niente' (*Fiabe italiane*, p. 644 and, with small variation, p. 728); 'Ed essi furono contenti e felici | E noi come mazzi di radici' (*Fiabe italiane*, p. 777).

> bracconiere, nei terreni gerbidi sotto il bosco; e poco dopo mio padre fu ucciso in una rissa, e la pellagra finì mia madre rimasta sola in quella misera capanna.
>
> (*Romanzi e racconti* I, 386)

The Sanremo landscape and the character-narrator are presented together at the beginning of the third chapter. For the sake of brevity I quote the passage describing the mood of patient expectation:

> Ogni nave che si vedeva allora, si diceva — Questo è Mastro Medardo che ritorna, — non perché fossimo impazienti che tornasse, ma tanto per aver qualcosa da aspettare,
>
> (*Romanzi e racconti* I, 376)

where the narrator seems to be the mouthpiece for the expectations of the whole community, which is a peaceful agricultural one:

> Il giorno avevamo vendemmiato e attraverso i filari vedevamo nel mare grigio avvicinarsi le vele d'una nave che batteva bandiera imperiale. [...] un giovane chiamato Fiorfiero, pigiando l'uva in cima al tino, gridò: — O, laggiù — ;
>
> (*Romanzi e racconti* I, 376)

Here again Calvino gives emphasis to the visual aspect, and the contrast between light and dark in the landscape adds to the pathos of Medardo's return:

> Fu di sera, già a buio; era ottobre; il cielo era coperto. Il giorno avevamo vendemmiato e attraverso i filari vedevamo nel mare grigio avvicinarsi le vele di una nave che batteva bandiera imperiale. [...] era quasi buio e vedemmo in fondovalle una fila di torce accendersi per la mulattiera; e poi, quando passò sul ponte distinguemmo una lettiga
>
> (*Romanzi e racconti* I, 376)

Furthermore, Medardo's village is actually called Terralba.[6] Here, too, Calvino avoids mentioning the names Sanremo or Liguria, which is surprising, considering that he not only names other regions, but even does so in ways that leave no doubt about the location of Terralba. Thus, for example, in connection with the alleged poachers cruelly punished as a result of il Gramo's verdict, the narrator informs us that they were 'cavalieri toscani che, diretti in Provenza passavano attraverso i nostri bordi' (*Romanzi e racconti* I, 383) and later, introducing the Huguenots, he says 'Era gente scappata d'in Francia [...] Nella traversata delle montagne [...] Così s'erano messi a coltivare le dure terre di Col Gerbido [...]' (*Romanzi e racconti* I, 395).

The narrator does not say much about Terralba as a town, but we know that there is a church without aisles (where the wedding ceremony takes place), a ruined castle with a courtyard and several towers, occupied initially by Medardo's family, and later just by il Gramo, with servants who survived the fire started by the owner himself; a carpenter's workshop, the undertaker's house and a cemetery, where Trelawney tries to ensnare the will-o'-the-wisps with his nets. The spatial relationship between these elements cannot be

6 Terralba is the name of the house where Mario Calvino, the author's father, was born on 26 March 1875.

deduced, since everything is left vague; the only certainty is that the vineyards and the sea can be seen from the castle.

All the rest, perhaps because of the historical setting, implies a rural economy. There are vineyards for the production, perhaps, of 'cancarone' wine (a Ligurian term, still in use, for poor quality wines and possibly an example of antonomasia); little wheat is grown (*Romanzi e racconti* I, 396), rye, maize, turnips and chick peas (*Romanzi e racconti* I, 428–29); there is a press (*Romanzi e racconti* I, 437) for the olives that are collected (as also in *Il barone rampante* for walnuts, *Romanzi e racconti* I, 744) by spreading sheets under the lowest branches of the olive trees (*Romanzi e racconti* I, 400). Horticulture is clearly an important feature: there is mention of courgettes (*Romanzi e racconti* I, 390), melons and tomatoes, which are even spread out to dry in the sun (*Romanzi e racconti* I, 424). The fruit trees mentioned are apple, pear, pomegranate (*Romanzi e racconti* I, 424) and fig (*Romanzi e racconti* I, 377 and 426).

Animal-rearing includes goats, pigs (*Romanzi e racconti* I, 378) and sheep (*Romanzi e racconti* I, 425); of cattle there is mention only of a bull (which il Gramo makes drunk on grappa, *Romanzi e racconti* I, 434). Reference is also made to donkeys, used to draw water from the wells (*Romanzi e racconti* I, 431), bees (*Romanzi e racconti* I, 405 and 408), rabbits (*Romanzi e racconti* I, 390) and poultry (*Romanzi e racconti* I, 407 and 424, but also Pamela's duck).

The woodland fauna is more revealing: Aiolfo's birds (pheasants, turtle doves, magpies, tits, shrike); squirrels, dormice, vipers, processionary moths and eels in the streams (*Romanzi e racconti* I, 414). The trees in the wood are mainly pines, but there are also mulberries (*Romanzi e racconti* I, 407), chestnuts (*Romanzi e racconti* I, 415) and raspberry bushes (*Romanzi e racconti* I, 395). In the undergrowth there are mushrooms: boleti, 'vescie', puffballs, agaric (*Romanzi e racconti* I, 381–82).

By contrast, the sea is unproductive and there is no mention of sea fishing; though we do hear of limpets, crabs, octopuses (*Romanzi e racconti* I, 402–03) and jellyfish (*Romanzi e racconti* I, 406). But it is also true that the unexpected and exotic emerges from the sea, with the turtle and the pineapples exhibited by the English sailors of Captain Cook (*Romanzi e racconti* I, 444) as evidence of a horizon broader than the immediate one.

There is talk of regional culinary habits, such as 'andare per pigne' (pine-nuts being a vital ingredient for 'pesto', *Romanzi e racconti* I, 438), eating slugs (*Romanzi e racconti* I, 423–24) and frying mushrooms (*Romanzi e racconti* I, 382).

I have brought together this information to show how detailed the story is and how it would be possible, theoretically, to locate the narrator's horizon even if it is anonymous. Nor does this richness of detail work against the generic mood typical of the fairy-tale because these are elements functional to the story, and such specialized description can also be seen in 'genuinely' popular fairy stories.[7] It is, however, true that in popular fairy stories the

[7] Compare, for example, the note at the end of Calvino's version of the popular Sicilian fairy-tale 'Sfortuna' (*Fiabe italiane*, p. 615) when he remarks how 'la genericità solita delle fiabe lasci il posto alla precisione linguistica e tecnica quando la Messia [the Sicilian teller whose version is reworked by Calvino] parla delle operazioni della lavandaia' (*Fiabe italiane*, pp. 864–65). Folktales may tend to offer stereotypical descriptions of aristocratic settings, but are all the more accurate when representing actions or settings close to the experience of the story-teller.

landscape is by convention generic — which explains the sparseness of information on Terralba as a town — and functional to the plot. In the case of *Il visconte dimezzato*, this is true above all when Medardo and/or Pamela appear centre stage. Description of the 'Prato delle monache' or the bridge 'della ghigna', despite the specificity of their names, is minimal. We learn that the former is a clearing with a pool in the middle — functional to the plot because in this pool il Gramo can contemplate the misleadingly whole reflection of the halves of the mushroom floating on the surface and look at himself without seeing himself as a whole, however misleadingly. About the latter, the bridge 'della ghigna', we are told that it is a duckboard construction between two crags — equally functional to the plot because it stages the second of il Gramo's three attempts to kill the narrator. The same is true as far as il Buono is concerned: the pond on whose banks the meeting with the narrator takes place is functional to the first three good deeds he carries out — replacing the eel with the ring, rescuing not only the narrator who is about to be stung by the red spider but also Trelawney who falls into the water and cannot swim. The same might be said of Pamela's adventures in the wood.

Now let us look at the more extreme treatment of the settings for the allegorical figures who, as 'Nota 1960' tells us, represent opposing attitudes towards literature, namely the Huguenots of Col Gerbido for commitment and the lepers of Pratofungo for escapism. It is easy enough to see Col Gerbido as corresponding to the estate of S. Giovanni, and Ezechiele to the author's father (see *La strada di San Giovanni*, *Romanzi e racconti* III, 7–26), which partly explains the greater characterization of the Huguenot setting. But the fact remains that one of the criteria for representation, that is, work in the fields, is inevitably more applicable to the Huguenots than to the lepers. Both communities have aspects that are atypical vis-à-vis the norm (Terralba). However, Col Gerbido has more markedly rural features while Pratofungo has to suggest a licentious sophistication which is completely alien to the norm.

It is interesting that Calvino also differentiates them in rural terms. While it is true that the lepers live on charity and do not have to work, even they do grow something ('Son tornati i giardinieri' is the cry on their return to Pratofungo, *Romanzi e racconti* I, 412). However, what they grow are strawberry grapes (uva fragola, *Romanzi e racconti* I, 391), jasmine (*Romanzi e racconti* I, 391), peppermint, rosemary, thyme (*Romanzi e racconti* I, 411), bay, hawthorn, anemones (*Romanzi e racconti* I, 412), oregano and mallow (*Romanzi e racconti* I, 413), marginal and superfluous items, aromatic herbs, vaguely transgressive and quite different, as Sebastiana explains, from the borage and cress whose infusions combat leprosy (*Romanzi e racconti* I, 413). In reality borage and cress are plants used in 'poor' Ligurian cooking.[8]

The Huguenots' agricultural model is hard-working and absolutely without frills, partly because of the earth itself, which consists of 'ripiani calcinosi dove a fatica cresceva qualche misera vite e dello stento frumento' (*Romanzi e racconti* I, 396); it is reached by a 'mulattiera

8 Discussing the story of Prezzemolina, Calvino explains how the initial alimentary transgression 'la scorpacciata di prezzemolo della donna incinta' is reminiscent of 'l'opposizione pianta alimentare — pianta aromatica [...] d'una botanica arcaica basata sull'opposizione alimento-aroma, agricoltura-giardinaggio, Cerere-Venere', in *Saggi* II, 1161–62.

sassosa' (*Romanzi e racconti* I, 426). The produce they do manage to cultivate is limited to olives, a yellow vine, figs, rye, rape, cattle fodder, wild endive, maize and chick peas (*Romanzi e racconti* I, 426–29).

All this may lead one to think that *Il visconte dimezzato* is a mere celebration of a narrow regional panorama and perhaps even more the idealization of an archaic and thus almost idyllic society, which would be far from doing justice to the text. As the already-quoted analysis of Bettelheim makes clear:

> The stories on the 'Two Brothers' theme add to this internal dialogue between id, ego and superego another dichotomy: the striving for independence and self-assertion, and the opposite tendency to remain safely home, tied to the parents. From the earliest version on, the stories stress that both desires reside in each of us, and that we cannot survive deprived of either: the wish to stay tied to the past, and the urge to reach out to a new future. Through the unfolding of events, the story most often teaches that entirely cutting oneself off from one's past leads to disaster, but that to exist only beholden to the past is stunting; while it is safe, it provides no life of one's own. Only the thorough integration of these contrary tendencies permits a successful existence.
>
> (Bettelheim 1975, p. 91)

Here we should look again at the Buono/Gramo dichotomy which characterizes the two parts of Medardo which, if they do not represent a moral contrast of a strictly Manichean type, do at all events represent polarities that we might define as conventionality and transgression in relation to the norm. Irrespective of the personal dissatisfaction of the two parts of the divided Medardo, his lack of wholeness makes him inefficient in terms of integration into society; that is, the transgressive part, il Gramo, also has some success, and the conventional part is highly inept, as his relationship with applied science shows, clearly represented by Mastro Pietrochiodo. At all events, what is stressed is that Medardo's action expresses scientific interests, traditionally regarded as progressive, and which initially can find little positive application.

Again, atypical societies also carry seeds of rebellion within them, as the figure of Esaù shows for the Huguenots and as the sense of alienation indicated by the nun's habit worn in protest by the wetnurse Sebastiana does among the lepers. But the escape of the narrator too is also a sign of rebellion, however inconclusive and passive. In this connection, we might consider the following quotation as a detail which broadens the polarization of the text to include the figure of the narrator in relation to the only other child in the story, Esaù:

> Questo modo di fare di Esaù non mi garbava, e quello dei suoi parenti mi metteva in soggezione. E allora preferivo starmene per conto mio e andare alla marina a raccogliere patelle e a cacciar granchi.
>
> (*Romanzi e racconti* I, 402)

The narrator and Esaù may be considered as brothers in the anthropological sense in that they are described as roughly of an age. In this way we may see the contrast between the behaviour of the two as further support for the hypothesis which suggests reading *Il visconte dimezzato* as part of the scheme of fairy stories which have two brothers as their protagonists. By entering the narrative as an orphan, the narrator is automatically put in a situation that demands a level of independence higher than that of his contemporary Esaù, and a more equal footing when dealing with adult characters. While Esaù's aggressive behaviour is clearly regressive, the narrator's escape into the playful world of imagination has liberating potential. Unlike the polarity between the two halves of Medardo, the polarity between these characters is left unresolved within the text. On a more crucial level, however, their features do merge, as they correspond to two recognizable self-portraits. On the one hand, Esaù is linked to the author by his own admission, as the association between the representation of the Huguenots and Calvino's family is stated in the 'Nota 1960' (*Romanzi e racconti* I, 1212). On the other, the characterization of the narrator as keen on looking for 'patelle' and with a father who was a hunter and used to live by those 'terreni gerbidi' near the wood reflects a typology of autobiographic representation which recurs in many of the narratives analysed in this book.

CHAPTER III

Echo Effects

The texts brought together and studied in this chapter, too, have much in common. They are relatively close chronologically, being composed over a period of eight years.[1] But in terms of the historical backgrounds which produced them, these books are the offspring of relatively different times. None of the three deals in any way overtly with the historical realities in which they saw the light of day, yet all three reflect their more obvious features. 'La formica argentina' appears to be a direct product of the historical disappointment of the Italian left in 1948 and, although the theme of the struggle against the excesses of nature may be said to be universal, the limited scope of the narrative, with its temporal and spatial limits which respect the three unities — time, space and action — of the classical theatre, calls to mind the narrow national outlook of the time, with an unpleasant taste to it, but undeniably home-grown. The same cannot be said of *Il barone rampante* or *La speculazione edilizia*, written after 1956, that is, when the Italians left had been painfully obliged to acknowledge not only the crimes of Stalin, and Soviet intervention in Hungary, but also the complexity of the problems of putting into effect Marxist ideology on an international level, even where it has already seemed a *fait accompli*. In view of the difficulty of assessing these events, it is natural that the intellectual autobiography which constitutes the backbone of the narrative should be more fitful, problematic and doubt-laden than in 'La formica argentina', where the same intellectual autobiography is no less intense, but far less complex.

The similarity between these texts is to be found on another level, which is not even that of literary genre. Unless we choose to regard them as fictional intellectual autobiographies, given the realistic-allegorical format of 'La formica argentina', the historical-fantastical format of *Il barone rampante* and the realist intellectual one of *La speculazione edilizia*, the three texts cannot be considered as belonging to the same genre.

However, even from the point of view of their autobiographical status, there are curious inconsistencies in Calvino's attitude to these texts: while in the introductory note to the school edition of *Il barone rampante* edited by the fictitious Tonio Cavilla (an anagram of the author's name), the writer stresses that the novel:

1 'La formica argentina' was begun in 1949 and finished in 1952, while the most recent work examined in this chapter, *La speculazione edilizia*, was written between 5 April 1956 and 12 July 1957. In reality these texts, which are relatively lengthy as against the average for Calvino's writings, overlap with others and exemplify his habitual tendency to vary genres and work on several desks. Particularly surprising is the closeness in time of writing between *La speculazione edilizia* and *Il barone rampante*, which was written between 10 December 1956 and 26 February 1957, during a break from the former.

> nasce da un'immagine legata ai ricordi infantili — il ragazzo che sale sull'albero — cioè ha la sua prima spinta nell'ambito lirico di quella «letteratura della memoria» che occupa tanto posto nella narrativa del Novecento,
>
> (*Romanzi e racconti* I, 1228)

on the other hand, the note which precedes the beginning of *La speculazione edilizia* maintains that:

> I luoghi, i fatti, le persone, i nomi di questo racconto sono assolutamente fantastici e non possono esservi trovati riferimenti con la realtà se non per caso.
>
> (*Romanzi e racconti* I, 780)

An examination of the editorial vicissitudes of this latter work, and the publication of a substantial corpus of the author's autograph letters, testify to the fact that it is an autobiographical text; yet the insertion of that paragraph is an attempt at denying as much.[2]

If, on the other hand, we consider the representation of the landscape, a basic compositional affinity soon becomes clear: by means of the emphasis of a single one of its elements — ants, trees and concrete respectively — the overall image of the landscape is rendered virtually unrecognizable. In these texts the author's descriptive procedure concerning the landscape is basically the same, and has the effect of modifying the pattern as a whole, through the detailed attention focused on one of its parts.

Thus the landscape, which should constitute a novelty for the narrator of 'La formica argentina', is thrust into second place by swarms of almost invisible ants. Similarly, the same landscape pattern sea-city-hills becomes an almost unbroken wooded expanse in *Il barone rampante* and an asphalt jungle in *La speculazione edilizia.*

This chapter looks at those works where one detail of the landscape has been repeated and diffused to the point of making the usual pattern sea-city-hills almost unrecognizable. The procedure is undoubtedly an expedient to avoid the background becoming monotonous, but it clearly charges it with other connotations. Thus one might say, for example, that the panorama of the bay as it appears in this group of works has been transformed into a garden of delights (or torments).

The difference between Eden and a garden of delights lies in the fact that while in the first one returns to a condition of prelapsarian innocence, in the second it is desire — and its opposite, fear — which, as an externalized element, becomes the 'place' where the hero undergoes a trial, since he has to prove that he is equal to the situation: in other words that he is spotless.

In the category of the 'marvellous', as in Eden, the world is benign and indeterminate, whereas the fantastic creates a world where desire, projected outwards, is mirrored everywhere: as for instance in the caves of crystal and oriental shish mahal, places regarded as

2 See *I libri degli altri. Lettere 1947–1981*, edited by G. Tesio (Turin, Einaudi, 1991), p. 419, in particular the letter to François Wahl from which it may be easily inferred that the insertion of the section already quoted into the beginning of *La speculazione edilizia* was dictated by the need to avoid further criticism from his friends from Sanremo portrayed in the story. Indeed, perhaps the over-categorical denial should have been understood as an affirmation from the start. For further clarification concerning the tortuous editorial history of the text, see both the note by Claudio Milanini in *Romanzi e racconti* I, 1338–51 and the analysis of the textual variants by Martin McLaughlin, 'Il "Fondo Italo Calvino"', *Autografo*, 17 (1989), 93–103.

sacred; but also in the power of the dream, according to the Freudian interpretation of its compensating function, which is found in a large number of fairy stories and popular tales: the witch's house in Hansel and Gretel, for example, with its reverse outside/inside polarity may be interpreted as a rendering of the ambivalent fantasies linked with the oral phase of the child's development.

This bipolarity of the fantastic and the theme of the trial are succinctly represented in one story, 'Pesci grossi, pesci piccoli' (*Romanzi e racconti* II, 983–92) though it is true that the whole Sanremo pattern does not occur, only the sea and the rocks.[3] In this tale the protagonist Zeffirino is haunted by a passion for underwater fishing and has acquired the necessary equipment:

> Quel giorno Zeffirino era riuscito a mettere insieme tutto l'armamento per la caccia subacquea. La maschera l'aveva già dall'anno scorso, regalo di sua nonna; una cugina che aveva i piedi piccoli gli prestò le pinne; il fucile lo prese a casa di suo zio senza dir niente e al padre disse che gliel'avevano prestato.
>
> (*Romanzi e racconti* II, 983–84)

Now he begins to pursue a whitebream which, just as certain magic deer or gazelles lead the hero into the wood, takes Zeffirino into a hollow amongst the rocks, peopled by droves of assorted fish.

> Era un posto ricchissimo di pesca, quasi uno specchio chiuso, e dovunque Zeffirino guardasse incontrava un guizzare di pinne sottili, luccichii di squame, tanto che dallo stupore e dalla gioia non gli venne di far partire quasi un colpo.
>
> (*Romanzi e racconti* II, 985)

The trial awaiting him has nothing to do with fishing: he has to console signorina De Magistris, a fat weeping siren, for her sufferings in love. The two characters are the mirror-image of each other, one being in ecstasy and the other in agony.

> Nello stesso momento, nello stesso posto esistevano due struggimenti così opposti e inconciliabili. Zeffirino non riusciva a pensarli entrambi insieme; né a lasciarsi andare all'uno o all'altro.
>
> (*Romanzi e racconti* II, 987)

The symmetry of the situation generates an impasse. The symbolic action in allegorical narrative, as Fletcher shows, may take the form either of progress or of battle; in the first case there is ritualistic and unilinear movement forward, in the second an effect of symmetry and balance, suggesting a stasis in the conflict (Fletcher 1964, pp. 146–59).[4]

Zeffirino tries to distract the weeping woman with his fishing, to make her share in his pleasure. He tries to project his enthusiasm. But she, too, projects her pain on to the fish that

[3] As further justification for the decision to include this story, we might mention Bruno Falcetto's note to 'La formica argentina', where we are told that in 1959 it appeared with the text in 'un'edizione fuori commercio corredata da illustrazioni di Franco Gentilini, nella collana di narrativa italiana diretta da Umbro Apollonio per il Sodalizio del libro di Venezia' (*Romanzi e racconti* I, 1312).

[4] A. Fletcher, *Allegory: The Theory of a Symbolic Mode* (Cornell University Press, 1964). Quoted from the 1982 edition, pp. 146–59. For another application of Fletcher's theory on Calvino's works see K. Hume, *Calvino's Fictions: Cogito and Cosmos* (Oxford, Clarendon Press, 1992), pp. 159–62.

have been caught, discovering in each of them traces of seagulls' beaks or water fleas gnawing at them under their scales. This is once again the 'pathos of distance': from a distance fish are fascinating, from close to they inspire pity. But through a sort of magic, created by desire, the phenomenon has undergone an effect of enlargement, of multiplication, or resonance; here we have the echo as amplifying system, whose effects on the characters have already been pointed out by Falaschi in relation to *Il sentiero dei nidi di ragno* (Falaschi 1976, p. 116), and which now also acts externally.

The garden of delights and the garden of torments are symmetrical and juxtaposed. The landscape, filtered through the characters' states of mind, is reduced to a minimum, to the enclosed hollow, to a short-sighted vision. One natural element is broadened and proliferates unduly (in accordance with the character's desire or fear).

We know that in allegory what counts is the hero's strength of mind, the upholding of his own convictions to the end. Those of the woman waver before the octopus: of all the creatures caught, it is the only one which does not fit in with her state of mind. To touch it is unwise, and yet it rescues her from the grip of her earlier melancholy. The octopus has the function of a magical creature, it performs the cathartic action which Zeffirino intended, but in an unexpected and incongruous way. Thus the image that Zeffirino receives of it from the water is all the more powerful:

> ... vide la donna grassa con il polpo che dal braccio allungava un tentacolo e la prendeva per la gola.
>
> (*Romanzi e racconti* II, 991)

The octopus is immediately sacrificed and, in a sudden, crucial transition from the fabulous to the low mimetic, it is offered to De Magistris 'per cucinarlo fritto'.

'La formica argentina'

In the introductory note to this chapter I defined this novella as realistic-allegorical. This was an attempt to square the clearly didactic aspect of the narrative with the prevalence of descriptive elements concerning a natural phenomenon, so unusual outside the Riviera Ligure, as to require particularly extensive description. The earliest readings of the text, however, unaware of the reality of the phenomenon described, saw the descriptive hyper-realism of the ant invasion, if not correctly, at least justifiably, as a component that distorted reality. For example, a critic as sophisticated and concise as François Wahl compares the phenomenon to 'un incubo kafkiano'[5] and the author himself, writing in the third person in the *Nota introduttiva* to *Gli Amori difficili*, stresses its estranging aspect:

> *La formica argentina* [...] lo si può ricollegare a quell'«icasticità figurativa di puro gusto gotico» nel rappresentare «l'orrido zoologico o botanico» di cui aveva parlato Emilio Cecchi a proposito del giovane Calvino
>
> (*Romanzi e racconti* II, 1291)

[5] F. Wahl, 'La logica dell'immagine in Calvino', *Il caffé*, 4 (1964), 36–37.

Pietro Ferrua was the first critic to point out that 'In un crescendo kafkiano, l'autore non fa altro che dar vita poetica ad una plaga ben nota della regione sanremese' (Ferrua 1977),[6] anticipating the very explanation contained in the author's letter to Goffredo Fofi, quoted in Bruno Falcetto's notes:

> *La formica argentina* non è onirico-kafkiana come hanno sempre detto tutti i critici. È il racconto più realistico che abbia mai scritto in vita mia; descrive con assoluta esattezza la situazione della invasione delle formiche argentine nelle coltivazioni a San Remo e in buona parte della Riviera di Ponente all'epoca della mia infanzia, anni Venti e anni Trenta.
>
> (*Romanzi e racconti* I, 1314)[7]

Despite the reality of the phenomenon described, the narrative is clearly allegorical in character. The protagonist's struggle against the evil of nature is presented through antithetical examples of behaviour which finally cease without the conflict being in any way resolved. Furthermore, if the key to a story is contained in the initial sentences, the register in which 'La formica argentina' should be read is that of the narrator's amazement when faced with the novel phenomenon. According to Todorov's classification, in the 'marvellous' the protagonist's initial amazement is not the norm: when it is manifested, it is a sign that we are on the borderline between the 'marvellous' and the 'fantastic' (Todorov 1970)[8] and the narrator's characterization as a newcomer is meant to underline his incredulity in the face of his new environment. From the narrator's point of view we can recognize three different phases in his relationship with the landscape: the first is desire, the idealization which has led him to make the journey to settle there with his family; the second is his gradual awareness of the problems present in this new world; the third is the discovery of a way of not allowing himself to be overwhelmed by them.

The narrator begins his story with his bewilderment in the face of the unexpected phenomenon. The theme of the journey and the search for a friendly natural environment are used to give this effect of surprise, but they remain outside the story: they are part of the past, they already belong to memory. For this reason, the characterization of the landscape before the discovery of the ants is very approximate and generic, and becomes careful and detailed only subsequently. The initial description is linked to the characterization of zio Augusto, a minor character who will vanish from the story almost immediately, having migrated to these parts before the narrator. It is a description that aims to emphasize a familiarity with local places and people such as the narrator also desires:

> Perché si fosse trovato bene, qui, nostro zio, cominciammo a intuirlo dalla prima sera, vedendo il chiarore dell'aria dopo cena e comprendendo il piacere di girare per quelle vie verso la campagna, sedersi sui muriccioli d'un ponte come vedemmo fare

6 P. Ferrua, 'Il sostrato sanremese nella narrativa di Italo Calvino', *Italica*, 54 (1977), 367–69.

7 Bruno Falcetto rightly underlines also 'l'unilateralità un po' paradossale e provocatoria' of the letter (*Romanzi e racconti* I, 1314). On the other hand though, even the traps to catch ants are not fictitious as documented in a long interview with Libereso Guglielmi in Ippolito Pizzetti, *Libereso: il giardiniere di Calvino* (Padua, Muzzio, 1993), pp. 117–18.

8 T. Todorov, *Introduction à la littérature fantastique* (Paris, Editions du Seuil, 1970).

> a certuni, e poi sempre di più quando trovammo un'osteria che lui aveva frequentato, con un orto dietro...
>
> (*Romanzi e racconti* I, 447)

Zio Augusto is free from all family ties, and hence untroubled by the ants; but the narrator, laden with responsibilities and worries, cannot escape the reality of the scourge.

The word 'formica', constantly repeated and stressed in this initial phase of the story, has to span the distance between its usual value and the circumstantial one. The exceptional nature of the phenomenon belongs to the natural order, and we are thus in the field of that 'ambiguity' described by Falaschi (1976, pp. 126 and ff.), with the discrepancy between the beauty of the countryside and the invincible nature of the plague of ants.

Although they are mentioned constantly, the ants are never described in detail, perhaps because, since they are part of everyone's experience, it would be hard to make them seem repulsive. But we infer that this is a particular species, smaller than usual and apparently totally gregarious in character, an impression possibly also given through the use of the collective singular, which makes it impossible for the reader to imagine them individually. To give an idea of the difference between the ordinary ant and the Argentine ant, the narrator uses a comparison which, though leaving the second species somewhat vague, nonetheless provides some idea of it:

> formiche? una formica avremmo visto, sperduta, una di quelle nostre formiche grasse (mi sembrano grasse ora le formiche dei nostri paesi)
>
> (*Romanzi e racconti* I, 447)

Apart from this, we know that they have a bitter smell and that they tickle unbearably when they crawl over the skin. Thus rather than of repugnance, they give a sense of uncontrollable unease; of obsession and frenzy rather than anxiety.

Almost invisible though they are, they still dominate the landscape; the attempts to combat them — whether with the captain's grotesque traps, the coloured trails of the Reginaudo's insecticide, the daubings of poisoned molasses provided by the State — are all signs of their insidious presence, which cannot be ignored:

> Ma per strada, già i posti mi sembravano diversi da ieri: in ogni orto, in ogni casa indovinavo le file di formiche che salivano sui muri, che coprivano gli alberi da frutto, che muovevano le antenne verso ogni cosa zuccherosa o grassa; e il mio occhio ormai sull'avviso scopriva subito le masserizie messe fuor di casa a sbattere perché le formiche le avevano invase, e il soffietto dell'insettifugo in mano a una vecchia, e il piattino di veleno, e, aguzzando gli occhi la fila che camminava imperturbabile, lungo il cornicione.
>
> (*Romanzi e racconti* I, 466–67)

If we choose so to call it, this too is the 'pathos of distance',[9] but this time rather than bringing relief, it sharpens the perception of the phenomenon, so that instead of detaching

9 See C. Cases, 'Calvino e il "pathos della distanza"', in *Città aperta*, 7–8 (1958), pp. 33–35, and in *I metodi attuali della critica in Italia*, edited by M. Corti and C. Segre (Turin, Eri/Edizioni Rai Radiotelevisione Italiana, 1970), pp. 53–58.

himself from it, the narrator feels beleaguered by it. The panorama of the bay is transformed into a nightmare, a garden of torments for whose possession human beings and ants contend. Thus even in his first walk with his wife, the two project from above a vision of themselves into the landscape below; they could equally not do so, they could forget it, but in fact they use their own imagination to keep it in mind, despite the fact that they suffer as a result:

> Mia moglie ed io salivamo per questo viale e giù dalle balaustre vedevamo la casetta dove abitavamo, ancora così poco a noi familiare, e la sterpaglia del terreno incolto, e il giardinetto dei Reginaudo simile al cortile di un magazzino, e il giardinetto dei Brauni con la sua compostezza quasi cimiteriale ed ecco che potevamo dimenticarci che erano luoghi neri di formiche, ecco ora potevamo vederli come sarebbero stati senza quell'assillo al quale non ci si poteva sottrarre neanche per un attimo, ecco ora a quella distanza potevano anche sembrare un paradiso — e però più dall'alto li guardavamo più ci prendeva un senso di pietà per la nostra vita laggiù, come se a vivere in quel meschino, gracile orizzonte, non si potesse che continuare a batterci contro problemi gracili e meschini.
>
> (*Romanzi e racconti* I, 474)

The horror with which Pin perceives what is close to him has here been joined by pity, 'sympathy' between man and nature. (In fact, of course, what signorina De Magistris had been feeling was also pity, despite the strongly caricatural tone in which it was expressed).

We have said that the narrator remains in a position of stalemate throughout the story, trying as he does to gain an idea of how to combat this scourge, unable to take up any definite stand. The story moves between opposing poles of behaviour, whose faults and virtues it illustrates and which it also rejects. In contrast to the narrator's inability to reach a decision, we have a description of the gradual crescendo of his wife's fury at the discovery that her son is crying desperately because an ant has got into his ear. Maternal anxiety for the child's well-being infects her husband and new women neighbours in a spiral of solidarity, frustrated rage and collective hysteria. Except that the solidarity is short-lived, and the little troop of women, with the narrator's wife at its head, which sets off to protest about the State molasses, breaks up en route, and the solidarity protest of the narrator's wife is interpreted as madness pure and simple. At this point, the satire becomes transparent: the blame for the failure to get the better of the ants is to be laid at the door of the state official and his molasses; indeed signor Baudino, successfully escaping in 'mosse sempre più formichesche', represents both the State and the perpetrator of the harm done. The women's behaviour, first enthusiastic, then cowardly, may be compared to the gradual cooling off of protests in the post-war period, and the narrator's disappointment at the behaviour of the new neighbours to that of the author at the result of the elections of 1948.

The narrator's frustration follows a logic of progressive negative reactions in a crescendo of bitterness, from outrage at the women's cowardice, to disgust at people who do nothing except complain, to a painful awareness that he cannot allow himself an aristocratic aloofness, until he finally comes somewhere near to an acceptance of reality without further illusions: 'Questo era il mio nuovo paese' (*Romanzi e racconti* I, 481).

It is the acceptance of reality which finally leads to action, to the decision to take a walk with his wife and child to look at the sea. Not that this will solve anything, but at least it leads the narrator to contemplate horizons free from ants and anthills; in the more overtly didactic logic which will shape the conclusion reached by Marco Polo in *Le città invisibili*, contemplation of the sea here represents the second method of avoiding the pains of hell:

> L'inferno dei viventi non è qualcosa che sarà; se ce n'è uno, è quello che è già qui, l'inferno che abitiamo tutti i giorni, che formiamo stando insieme. Due modi ci sono per non soffrirne. Il primo riesce facile a molti: accettare l'inferno e diventarne parte fino al punto di non vederlo più. Il secondo è rischioso e richiede attenzione e apprendimento continui: cercare e sapere riconoscere chi e cosa, in mezzo all'inferno, non è inferno, e farlo durare e dargli spazio.
>
> (*Romanzi e racconti* II, 498)

The description of the walk to the sea taken by the narrator and his wife marks a total change of register in relation to the rest of the story. The wonder of the child's gaze as it contemplates the still unfamiliar countryside communicates itself to the adult narrator:

> Nostro figlio si voltava stupito a vedere ogni cosa e a noi toccava prendere parte alla sua meraviglia.
>
> (*Romanzi e racconti* I, 481)

However, the gaze which lingers on a section of the old town, lit by the setting sun, is a special gaze:

> Era sera. Passavamo per viali e strade a scale. Il sole batteva su uno spigolo della città vecchia, di pietra grigia e porosa, con cornici di calce alle finestre e i tetti verdi d'erba. Nell'entroterra la città si apriva a ventaglio, s'ondulava in versanti di colline, e dall'uno all'altro spazio era colmo d'aria limpida, a quest'ora color rame.
>
> (*Romanzi e racconti* I, 481)

But this partial view of the old town, etched by the sunlight, becomes peopled with vaguely surreal vignettes. Elusive, purely descriptive, incongruous, they occur irrespective of judgement, as in a silent film:

> Incontrammo delle donne anziane che portavano grandi ceste in bilico sul capo posate sopra un cercine — camminavano immobili, col torso fermo sulle reni, gli occhi bassi —; e da un giardino di monache un gruppo di ragazze cucitrici corsero a una ringhiera per vedere un rospo in una vasca e dissero: — Oh che angoscia! — e dietro un cancello, sotto un glicine, delle giovinette biancovestite facevano giocare con un pallone da spiaggia un cieco; e un ragazzo mezzo nudo e barbuto, coi capelli fino alle spalle, coglieva i fichi d'India con una canna aperta a forchetta da una vecchia pianta irta di spine lunghe e candide; e i bambini di una casa ricca, tristi e occhialuti, facevano bolle di sapone alla finestra; ed era l'ora che ai vecchi del ricovero suona la ritirata e salivano per quelle scale l'uno dietro l'altro col bastone, con la paglietta in capo, parlando ciascuno per suo conto; e allora dei due operai del telefono quello che teneva la scala disse a quello controluce sui fili: — Scendi, è ora, domani finiremo.
>
> (*Romanzi e racconti* I, 481–82)

The observer has gone beyond the boundaries of his own personal concerns, he has gone beyond the ego, he is not trying to find causal links between one scene and the other. Finally this gaze will be fixed upon the sea, on the great stretches of water, on the colours of the waves, and our thoughts turn to the smoothing process which the currents work upon the shells. The words, the interest of this narrator, obsessed with the ants' indominable will, ends in a vision of natural beauty, a sort of cosmic embracing of the elements: the sea, understood as the maternal womb, from a Freudian perspective, retains the fascination of a life which extends to times both before birth and after death:

> Così arrivammo al porto e c'era il mare. C'era una fila di palme, e delle panche in pietra: io e mia moglie sedemmo e il bambino era quieto. Mia moglie disse: — Qui non c'è formiche —. Io dissi: — E c'è un bel fresco: si sta bene.
>
> Il mare andava su e giù contro gli scogli del molo, muovendo quelle barche dette 'gozzi', e uomini dalla pelle oscura le riempivano di rosse reti e nasse per la pesca serale. L'acqua era calma, con appena uno scambiarsi continuo di colori, azzurro e nero, sempre più fitto quanto più lontano. Io pensavo alle distanze d'acqua così, agli infiniti granelli di sabbia sottile giù nel fondo, dove la corrente posa gusci bianchi di conchiglie puliti dalle onde.
>
> (*Romanzi e racconti* I, 482)

Il barone rampante

The bewitched remoteness seen in the previous quotation leads us on to Cosimo's first scanning of the world from the top of the trees, after his rebellion, in *Il barone rampante*:

> Mio fratello stava come di vedetta. Guardava tutto, e tutto era come niente. Tra i limoneti passava una donna con un cesto. Saliva un mulattiere per la china, reggendosi alla coda della mula. Non si videro tra loro; la donna al rumore degli zoccoli ferrati, si voltò e si sporse verso strada, ma non fece in tempo. Si mise a cantare allora, ma il mulattiere passava già alla svolta, tese l'orecchio, schioccò la frusta e alla mula disse, — Aah! — E tutto finì lì. Cosimo vedeva questo e quello.
>
> (*Romanzi e racconti* I, 560–61)

Such a dispassionate vision befits the person who has found an inner measure, that is, the right way of being himself and of being in the world, a central metaphor in this highly successful allegory, entirely set in the open air, in a Ligurian landscape embellished, for the occasion, with trees of all kinds:

> Più in là le chiome degli alberi si sfittivano e l'ortaglia digradava in piccoli campi a scala, sostenuti da muri di pietre; il dosso era scuro di oliveti e, dietro, l'abitato d'Ombrosa sporgeva i suoi tetti di marrone sbiadito e ardesia, e ne spuntavano pennoni di bastimenti, là dove sotto c'era il porto. In fondo si stendeva il mare, alto d'orizzonte, ed un lento veliero vi passava.
>
> (*Romanzi e racconti* I, 560)

Ombrosa corresponds to a longed-for eighteenth-century Sanremo deep in woodland, a landscape which at the moment when it was described by the narrator had already ceased to exist, having been destroyed by the infamous profit motive, from the Napoleonic wars onwards (*Romanzi e racconti* I, 577).

The nostalgic vein evident in the words of Biagio, alone in the unrecognizable countryside, is firmly contained. In so far as it is made explicit both at the beginning of chapter IV and in the epilogue, it serves as a framework for the greater part of the narrative. A central position is occupied by the enthusiasm dominating Cosimo's life of exploration of the arboreal world, and by the beautiful descriptions at the beginning of the fourth and tenth chapters in a growing familiarity with the 'universo di linfa' (*Romanzi e racconti* I, 578) in which the character is immersed:[10]

> Allora, dovunque s'andasse, avevamo sempre rami e fronde tra noi e il cielo. L'unica zona di vegetazione più bassa erano i limoneti, ma anche là in mezzo si levavano contorti gli alberi di fico, più a monte ingombravano tutto il cielo degli orti, con le cupole del pesante loro fogliame, e se non erano fichi erano ciliegi dalle brune fronde, o più teneri cotogni, peschi, mandorli, giovani peri, prodighi susini e poi sorbi, carrubi, quando non era un gelso o un noce annoso. Finiti gli orti, cominciava l'oliveto, grigio-argento, una nuvola che sbiocca a mezza costa. In fondo c'era il paese accatastato, tra il porto in basso e in su la rocca; ed anche lì, tra i tetti, un continuo spuntare di chiome di piante: lecci, platani, anche roveri, una vegetazione più disinteressata e altera che prendeva sfogo — un ordinato sfogo — nella zona dove i nobili avevano costruito le ville e cinto di cancelli i loro parchi. Sopra gli olivi cominciava il bosco. I pini dovevano un tempo aver regnato su tutta la plaga, perché ancora s'infiltravano in lami e ciuffi di bosco giù per i versanti fino alla spiaggia del mare, e così i larici. Le roveri erano più frequenti e fitte di quanto oggi non sembri, perché furono la prima e più pregiata vittima della scure. Più in su i pini cedevano ai castagni, il bosco saliva la montagna e non se ne vedevano i confini.
>
> (*Romanzi e racconti* I, 577–78)

Transformed into an idyllic eighteenth-century landscape, the panorama of the bay is not completely idealized, nor lacking in desolate areas, as the description of Porta Capperi reveals: here, between the little figures of townsfolk clearly inspired by the eighteenth-century pictorial representations of the *Bamboccianti*,[11] we can easily recognize the equivalent of the Città Vecchia:

> Ora i monelli sono arrivati a Porta Capperi, guarnita di cascate verdi di capperi giù per le mura. Dalle catapecchie intorno viene un gridìo di madri. Ma questi sono bambini che la sera le madri non gridano per farli tornare, ma perché sono tornati, invece di cercarsi da mangiare altrove. Attorno a Porta Capperi, in casupole e

[10] Here we may note a similarity with the description of the passion for botany, technical names and taxonomy attributed to his father in *La strada di San Giovanni* in *Romanzi e racconti* III, 9 in the quotation on p. 74.

[11] *Bambocciate* is the name given to the popular genre of urban paintings introduced in Rome by Pieter van Laer and his followers, nicknamed *Bamboccianti*. The genre which became successful before the 1640s was practised mainly by northerners and depicted minute and intimate episodes of humble street life. See R. Wittkower, *Art and Architecture in Italy 1600–1750* (London, Pelican, 1982), p. 323 and G. Briganti, L. Trezzani and L. Laureati, *I Bamboccianti* (Roma, Bozzi, 1983); for related considerations see also M. Belpoliti, *Storie del visibile: Lettura di Italo Calvino* (Rimini, Luisè, 1990), pp. 81–83. The descriptive detail in which mothers call their children home in the evening recurs elsewhere, especially in *Il sentiero dei nidi di ragno* (*Romanzi e racconti* I, 10) and *La strada di San Giovanni* (*Romanzi e racconti* III, 9).

> baracche d'assi, carrozzoni zoppicanti, tende, era assiepata la gente più povera d'Ombrosa, così povera da essere tenuta fuori dalle porte della città e lontana dalle campagne, gente sciamata via da terre e paesi lontani, cacciata dalla carestia e dalla miseria che s'espandeva in ogni Stato. Era il tramonto e donne spettinate con bimbi al seno sventolavano fornelli fumosi, e mendicanti si stendevano al fresco sbendando le piaghe, altri giocando a dadi con rotti urli. I compagni della banda della frutta ora si mischiavano a quel fumo di frittura e a quegli alterchi, prendevano manrovesci dalle madri, s'azzuffavano tra loro rotolando nella polvere. E già i loro stracci avevano preso il colore di tutti gli altri stracci, e la loro allegria da uccelli invischiata in quell'aggrumarsi umano si sfaceva in una densa insulsaggine.
>
> (*Romanzi e racconti* I, 592–93)

But the description of the built-up area of Ombrosa is pared down to the minimum: rather, as in *Il visconte dimezzato*, the mention of public buildings is strictly functional to the story. The image of Cosimo up on the holm oak, and framed by the open window of the cathedral, appears fleetingly to represent his gradual withdrawal from the rituals of civic living (*Romanzi e racconti* I, 629); the cemetery is linked to his father's funeral, and the narrator stresses that Cosimo's enforced distance from it while he contemplates his burial is equivalent to the distance which has always existed between his father and the rest of the family (*Romanzi e racconti* I, 674); Cosimo manages to tap on the window of the bookseller Orbecche from the branches of a carob tree (*Romanzi e racconti* I, 643); he reads aloud first *Clarissa* and then *Jonathan Wild* from a clump of cluster pines to Gian dei Brughi, locked in the prison of Ombrosa, a small tower on the sea shore (*Romanzi e racconti* I, 648–49); a tall oak in the town square acts as the local gallows (*Romanzi e racconti* I, 649) and right in the middle of the square stands a walnut tree, the last tree to be climbed by the baron just before his death (*Romanzi e racconti* I, 773–75).

Most of the narrative is set in the coastal strip amidst the woods and villas which stand above the town and the perspective from which Cosimo observes the world is immersed in nature. But the impression is still that of a view from above, whose furthest limit, for both the ear and the eye, is constituted by the sea:

> Era il mondo ormai a essergli diverso, fatto di stretti e ricurvi ponti del vuoto, di nodi o scaglie o rughe che irruvidiscono le scorze, di luci che variano il loro verde a seconda del velario di foglie più fitte o più rade, tremanti al primo scuotersi d'aria sui peduncoli o mosse come vele all'incurvarsi dell'albero. Mentre il nostro, di mondo, s'appiattiva là in fondo, e noi avevamo figure sproporzionate e certo nulla capivamo di quello che lui lassù sapeva, lui che passava la notte ad ascoltare come il legno stipa delle sue cellule i giri che segnano gli anni nell'interno dei tronchi, e le muffe allargano la chiazza al vento tramontano, e in un brivido gli uccelli addormentati dentro il nido rincantucciano il capo là dove più morbida è la piuma dell'ala e si sveglia il bruco e si schiude l'uovo dell'averla. C'è il momento in cui il silenzio della campagna si compone nel cavo dell'orecchio in un pulviscolo di rumori, un gracchio, uno squittio, un fruscio velocissimo tra l'erba, uno schiocco nell'acqua, un zampettio tra terra e sassi, e lo strido della cicala alto su tutto. I rumori si tirano uno con l'altro, l'udito arriva a sceverarne sempre di nuovi come

> alle dita che disfano un bioccolo di lana ogni stame si rivela intrecciato di fili sempre più sottili ed impalpabili. Le rane intanto continuano il gracidio che resta nello sfondo e non muta il flusso dei suoni, come la luce non varia per il continuo ammicco delle stelle. Invece a ogni levarsi o scorrere via del vento, ogni rumore cambiava ed era nuovo. Solo restava nel cavo più profondo dell'orecchio l'ombra di un mugghio o murmure: era il mare.
>
> (*Romanzi e racconti* I, 620)

Again there are references to an instinctive world which reifies desire: the tree which acts as a 'stepping stone' between the familiar and domestic world of his father's villa and the park of the D'Ondariva is the scented and seductive magnolia (*Romanzi e racconti* I, 562); the background against which Viola moves is an exotic garden, mysteriously planted with every species of tree (*Romanzi e racconti* I, 562); during the period of arson even the night sky is lit up by the glitter of incandescent stars (*Romanzi e racconti* I, 658); Ursula, the noble Spanish damsel on whom Cosimo bestows his first kiss on 'un mandorlo tenero e non vasto' (*Romanzi e racconti* I, 684), is the object of a brief and tender adolescent passion which burgeons amidst the spring flowering of the branches (*Romanzi e racconti* I, 685). The relationship between man and nature is absolutely central; Cosimo's growing familiarity with the wood begins with a self-quotation, with the episode of the boy who finds himself sitting near a blackbird which he did not notice until it flew away (*Romanzi e racconti* I, 561 and 51).

Yet with all his love — or, as Calvino would say, because of all his love — Cosimo is not an 'idealized' figure, he is no noble savage: at first the toes of his shoes graze the branches of soft wood, 'aprendo bianche ferite nel nero della scorza' (*Romanzi e racconti* I, 562). Later he will solve the problem by wearing slippers, because the difference between Cosimo and later generations as portrayed in the text lies precisely in his greater degree of awareness, in the sense of responsibility at the root of his behaviour. Whether we choose to interpret his superior thoughtfulness as a tribute to the power of reason of the Enlightment or as a feature peculiar to intellectuals, the stress of the narrative is on the hardships and personal cost of this learning process. Similarly, he will later learn the art of tree-pruning and, as Biagio will comment:

> Insomma l'amore per questo suo elemento arboreo seppe farlo diventare, com'è di tutti gli amori veri, anche spietato e doloroso, che ferisce e recide per far crescere e dar forma.
>
> (*Romanzi e racconti* I, 655)

The same applies to hunting, a youthful passion which he will also repudiate over time, though the narrator continues to imply that his first instinct was perhaps more healthy than the subsequent one (*Romanzi e racconti* I, 735–37).[12]

[12] See the description of the author's father's passion for hunting in *La strada di San Giovanni*: 'Ma al di là delle fasce coltivate, uno squittire, un frullo, uno smuovere d'erba, bastava a fargli alzare di scatto i tondi fissi occhi e la barbetta appuntita, restare a orecchio teso, (aveva un viso fermo da gufo, con scatti talora come un rapace da preda, aquila o condor), e già non era più l'uomo dei campi, ma l'uomo dei boschi, il cacciatore, perché questa era la sua passione — la prima, sì, la prima, ossia l'ultima, l'estrema forma della sua passione [...]' (*Romanzi e racconti* III, 10).

The love between Cosimo and his 'element' is thus uninhibited and passionate: the wood brings together all his anxieties, from those which are still childish, as when he climbs unseeing, without looking around him (*Romanzi e racconti* I, 586), to adult ones where the very way he climbs denotes dissatisfaction with himself:

> Non sapeva neanche lui cosa voleva: preso dalle sue furie s'arrampicava rapidissimo sulle vette più tenere e fragili, come se cercasse altri alberi che crescessero sulla cima degli alberi per salire anche su quelli.
>
> (*Romanzi e racconti* I, 701)

Elsewhere his manner of climbing serves as a prelude to erotic desire; see for instance the following passage placed as an introduction to a catalogue of sexual encounters:

> Pareva preda a un'irrequietudine da uccello: saltava di ramo in ramo, ficcanaso, ombroso, inconcludente.
>
> (*Romanzi e racconti* I, 691)

In a similar fashion mad scamperings from branch to branch express his enthusiasm at Viola's return:

> Cosimo si gettò nel folto; avrebbe voluto che fosse mille volte più folto, una valanga di foglie rami e spine e caprifogli e capelveneri da affondarci e sprofondarci e solo dopo essercisi del tutto sommerso cominciare a capire se era felice o folle di paura.
>
> (*Romanzi e racconti* I, 710)

Such frenzy is followed by the bitter pain of Viola's desertion, which turns Cosimo into an eighteenth-century version of Orlando, though here method replaces brute force:

> Poi venne il tempo della violenza distruggitrice: ogni albero cominciava dalla vetta e, via una foglia via l'altra, rapidissimo lo riduceva bruco come d'inverno anche se non era d'abito spogliante. Poi risaliva in cima e tutti i ramoscelli li spezzava finché non lasciava che grosse travature, risaliva ancora e con un temperino cominciava a staccare la corteccia, e si vedevano le piante scorticate scoprire il bianco con abbrividente aria ferita.
>
> (*Romanzi e racconti* I, 733)

This destructive phase is followed by spells of madness, mid-way between elation and incoherence, when he tries to recover from his pain by preaching and declaiming from the treetops, covered with feathers, declaring himself now 'pettirosso', now a 'barbagianni', now a 'codibugnolo' (*Romanzi e racconti* I, 735). Visually, his madness is expressed through senseless decorations:

> I suoi alberi ora erano addobbati di fogli scritti e anche di cartelli con massime di Seneca e di Shaftesbury, e di oggetti: ciuffi di penne, ceri da chiesa, falciuole, corone, busti da donna, pistole, bilance, legati l'uno all'altro in un certo ordine.
>
> (*Romanzi e racconti* I, 736)

Cosimo spends his time amidst the darkness of the trees, but again it is interesting that there are three large-scale general views, three panoramic broadenings-out corresponding to the moments of greatest narrative pathos: the already-quoted initial wonder at the view from the treetop, the beginning of the love affair with Viola, and lastly his death. Each one of them indicates a new phase in the narrative like an unexpected development. See, for example, the element of surprise in the middle scene with Viola:

> — Di qua, — e andavano su certi olivi, protesi da una ripida erta, e dalla vetta d'uno di essi il mare che finora scorgevano solo frammento per frammento tra foglie e rami come frantumato, adesso tutt'a un tratto lo scopersero calmo e limpido e vasto come il cielo. L'orizzonte si apriva largo ed alto e l'azzurro era teso e sgombro senza una vela e ci si contavano le increspature appena accennate delle onde. Solo un lievissimo risucchio, come un sospiro, correva per i sassi della riva.
>
> (*Romanzi e racconti* I, 712)

Surprise is also the main feature of Cosimo's death, his final disappearance into the landscape:

> L'agonizzante Cosimo, nel momento in cui la fune dell'ancora gli passò vicino, spiccò un balzo di quelli che gli erano consueti nella sua gioventù, s'aggrappò alla corda, coi piedi ancora sull'ancora e il corpo raggomitolato, e così lo vedemmo volar via, trascinato nel vento, frenando appena la corsa del pallone, e sparire verso il mare...
>
> La mongolfiera, attraversato il golfo riuscì ad atterrare poi sull'altra riva. Appesa alla corda c'era solo l'ancora. Gli aeronauti, troppo affannati a cercare di tenere una rotta, non s'erano accorti di nulla. Si suppose che il vecchio morente fosse sparito mentre volava in mezzo al golfo.
>
> (*Romanzi e racconti* I, 776)

With Cosimo's departure, before the end of the narrative, the panorama of Ombrosa dissolves before Biagio's eyes, and his anxiety about a bay without woods begins:

> Ogni tanto scrivendo m'interrompo e vado alla finestra. Il cielo è vuoto e a noi vecchi d'Ombrosa, abitutati a vivere sotto quelle verdi cupole, fa male agli occhi guardarlo. Si direbbe che gli alberi non hanno retto, dopo che mio fratello se n'è andato o che gli uomini sono stati presi dalla furia della scure.
>
> (*Romanzi e racconti* I, 776)

This is the end of the Utopia, the end of the dream. To find a new balance between the positive and negative values of the imaginary, when the adventures of the baron are over, Calvino will go back to a symmetric endeavour in *La speculazione edilizia*, trying to discover the true nature of 'la furia della scure' which has destroyed Ombrosa.

La speculazione edilizia

Calvino himself tells us about the method he used in writing *La speculazione edilizia*:

> Per dare il senso di come il nostro tempo si muove e avere una coscienza completa di ogni processo degenerativo, sento il bisogno di un atteggiamento che definirei «mimesi attiva della negatività»; cioè trasportarci violentemente dalla parte di ogni

> fenomeno, ogni modo di pensare che giudichiamo negativo, entrare nella sua logica interna portandola alle ultime conseguenze, vivere insomma la negatività «al grado eroico». Finora sono riuscito a farlo solo ne *La speculazione edilizia*, dove un intellettuale costringe se stesso a entusiasmarsi di ciò che sommamente odia, la febbre di nuove costruzioni che sta mutando il volto alla Riviera, e a lanciarsi in disastrosi affari di aree fabbricabili. Vittorini ha definito «neo-balzacchiano» questo atteggiamento. Difatti Balzac, di fronte alla nascente borghesia degli affari, pur odiandola ideologicamente, ne faceva vivere lo slancio ai suoi eroi, e ce ne creava così un'immagine di verità ineguagliabile.
>
> (*Saggi* II, 2722–23)

Thus, for Calvino, the return to the realistic Sanremo becomes charged with a desire for self-injury, the price to be paid so that the character of Quinto Anfossi may be in step with the times. Thus we should say immediately that the hilltop view inevitably disappears from the narrative, while the view from down in the town remains, always stopping at the nearby, new wave of concrete:

> Sua madre, ogni volta che lui veniva a ***, per prima cosa lo faceva salire sul terrazzo, (lui, con la sua nostalgia pigra, distratta e subito disappetente sarebbe ripartito senz'andarci); — Adesso ti faccio vedere le novità, — e gli indicava le nuove fabbriche: — Là i Sampieri soprelevano, quello è un palazzo nuovo di certi di Novara, e le monache, anche le monache, ti ricordi il giardino coi bambù che si vedeva là sotto? Ora guarda che scavo, chissà quanti piani vogliono fare con quelle fondamenta! E l'araucaria della villa Van Moen, la più bella della Riviera, adesso l'impresa Baudino ha comprato tutta l'area, una pianta che avrebbe dovuto preoccuparsene il Comune, andata in legno da bruciare; del resto, trapiantarla era impossibile, le radici chissadove arrivavano. Vieni da questa parte, ora; qui a levante, vista da toglierci non ne avevamo più, ma guarda quel nuovo tetto che è spuntato: ebbene adesso il sole alla mattina arriva qui mezz'ora dopo.
>
> (*Romanzi e racconti* I, 782)

Thus, spatially, a sense of gloomy claustrophobia is produced, which contrasts with the free-roaming gaze of Quinto's memory:

> Quando Quinto saliva alla sua villa, un tempo dominante la distesa dei tetti della città nuova e i bassi quartieri della marina e del porto, più in qua i mucchi delle case muffite e lichenose della città vecchia, tra il versante della collina a ponente dove sopra gli orti s'infittiva l'oliveto, e, a levante, un reame di ville e alberghi verdi come un bosco, sotto il dosso brullo dei campi di garofani scintillanti di serre fino al Capo: ora più nulla, non vedeva che un sovrapporsi geometrico di parallelepipedi e poliedri, spigoli e lati di case, di qua e di là, tetti, finestre, muri ciechi per servitù contigue con solo i finestrini smerigliati dei gabinetti uno sopra l'altro.
>
> (*Romanzi e racconti* I, 782)

Quinto's claustrophobia tallies with his sophisticated and discontented way of reasoning, that of a disappointed and over-clever intellectual. For him as a habitual traveller who raises his eyes from his book in the train, the gloom of the new concrete is grimly acknowledged as an obstacle between past and present. This visual change is linked with other unpleasant developments. For Quinto this means the withdrawal of an old and decent urban city bourgeoisie in favour of a band of newcomers with neither scruples nor any sense of responsibility; and therefore the advance of an amoral cynicism, of short-sighted greed, of total insensitivity:

> Però ogni volta c'era qualcosa che gli interrompeva il piacere di quest'esercizio e lo faceva tornare alle righe del libro, un fastidio che non sapeva bene neanche lui. Erano le case: tutti questi nuovi fabbricati che tiravano su, casamenti cittadini di sei otto piani, a biancheggiare massicci come barriere di rincalzo al franante digradare della costa, affacciando più finestre e balconi che potevano verso mare. La febbre del cemento s'era impadronita della Riviera: là vedevi il palazzo già abitato con le cassette dei gerani tutti uguali ai balconi, qua il caseggiato appena finito, coi vetri segnati da serpenti di gesso, che attendeva le famigliole lombarde smaniose di bagni; più in là ancora un castello d'impalcature e, sotto, la betoniera che gira e il cartello dell'agenzia per l'acquisto dei locali.
>
> (*Romanzi e racconti* I, 781)

The change of the landscape is described as utter destruction of a serene and innocent way of life when the narrator focuses on Quinto's city:

> Nelle cittadine in salita, a ripiani, gli edifizi nuovi facevano a chi monta sulle spalle dell'altro, e in mezzo i padroni delle case vecchie allungavano il collo nei soprelevamenti. A ***, la città di Quinto, un tempo circondata da giardini ombrosi d'eucalipti e magnolie dove tra siepe e siepe vecchi colonnelli inglesi e anziane miss si prestavano edizioni Tauchnitz e annaffiatoi, ora le scavatrici ribaltavano il terreno fatto morbido dalle foglie marcite o granulose dalle ghiaie dei vialetti, e il piccone diroccava le villette a due piani, e la scure abbatteva in uno scroscio cartaceo i ventagli delle palme Washingtonia, dal cielo dove si sarebbero affacciate le future soleggiate-tricamere-servizi.
>
> (*Romanzi e racconti* I, 782)

Quinto's mother represents all these declining values, remote as she is from the rhetoric of complaints or scandalized comments. She, on the contrary, feels 'il rimpianto per un paesaggio caro che moriva' (*Romanzi e racconti* I, 783); she is close to the earth, and invests much of her time and affections in cultivating the beauty of her plants.[13]

[13] Just as the first-person narrator is a representation of the author distorted in a negative sense, so the portrait of the mother is totally positive and seems to be a tribute to Eva Mameli Calvino. The recurrent interweaving of distance and solicitude is not unlike that of Cosimo in his relations to Konradine von Kurtewitz in *Il barone rampante*, where both the name and the portrait of the mother is affectionately caricatural; indeed in 'Autobiografia Politica Giovanile', now in *Saggi* II, 2733–59, we discover that the author's mother was a convinced pacifist, albeit in a soldierly way: 'Ai tempi del Fronte Popolare in Francia, nostra madre all'ora della merenda ci faceva mettere sull'attenti guardando verso Oriente e dire: «Pour le pain, pour la paix, pour la liberté»' (p. 2739). In *La strada di san Giovanni*, the figure of the mother is conveyed through the narrator's inability properly to recall her voice, and his need rather to stress 'un suo dominio silenzioso' in *Romanzi e racconti* III, 14. Calvino's relations to his mother are also described as 'intensi e silenziosi' also in Silvio Dian's

Thus it is the polemical clash of these values, already regretted as irredeemably lost, which drives Quinto to undertake his adventures as a speculator, but it is also a desire to establish his realistic and tangible importance, to regain his own position in urban activities, to become part of the anti-aesthetic and amoral actions typical of the present, to seek an involvement in horrendous bureaucratic intrigues which culminates in the choice of the worst possible partner.

In this story, historical considerations occupy considerable space, more space than the descriptive passages. The concrete springs up everywhere, in particular at the beginning of the book, then becomes the tip of the iceberg of the amoral human relations which underlie it, in a crescendo of disgust and dissatisfaction with the present.

In reality, Anfossi's problems are only partly new; in addition to the present, the recent past, too, is disagreeable, and once again the unease is expressed in spatial terms:

> Per andare dal notaio doveva percorrere un tratto della via principale, che di solito, per una sua confusa remora, evitava. Nei suoi ritorni a *** sceglieva sempre itinerari mezzo in campagna o lungo la marina, dove c'erano da riscoprire sensazioni d'una memoria più sedimentata, marginale o minore. In città no, tutto era brutto, la memoria era un tritume di fatti quotidiani. Poi non sapeva mai chi salutare e chi no: a un certo punto della sua giovinezza aveva rotto con tutti, s'era iscritto al partito comunista, s'era fatto tutti nemici; e quelli che aveva avuto allora compagni, peggio, gli pareva che adesso dovessero avercela con lui anche più degli altri. Ora neppure la nostalgia del vecchio mondo che sparisce agiva in lui; vista da quei marciapiedi la città era uguale a sempre, straziantemente uguale, e quel che c'era di nuovo — facce, gioventù, negozi — non contava nulla, il tempo dell'adolescenza pareva sgradevolmente vicino. Cosa gli era preso, di riattaccarsi a ***? Quinto adesso voleva solo sbrigare in fretta quelle pratiche e partire. Decisamente stare a *** lo riempiva di fastidio.
>
> (*Romanzi e racconti* I, 799)

It is interesting to see how Calvino tried to answer once again this same question in the last three works considered: how to associate with other men to join common battle. The historical question is resolved in different ways, ranging from the angry and solitary realization of the narrator of 'La formica argentina', through the radiant exemplariness of the behaviour of Cosimo, to the bitter challenge faced by Quinto Anfossi. In this connection, Germana Pescio Bottino talks of a clear and gradual tendency towards anarchism in Calvino's thinking (Pescio Bottino 1976, p. 70).[14] This theory is sustainable, particularly if

---

'Testimonianza' in *Calvino, la letteratura, la scienza, la città: Proceedings of the Conference of Sanremo 1986*, edited by G. Bertone (Genoa, Marietti, 1988), pp. 136–37 and republished in Elisabetta Mondello, *Italo Calvino* (Pordenone, Studio Tesi, 1990), pp. 145–47. Calvino admiringly recalls his mother's outstanding courage during the Nazi-fascist occupation of Sanremo on several occasions; see in particular *Saggi* II, 2746 and 2913. The boys he was at school with, and the friends he made in early youth also remember Eva Mameli Calvino as a deeply committed scholar and a woman of great courage; see Ippolito Pizzetti, *Libereso: il giardiniere di Calvino* (Padua, Muzio, 1993). For an intelligent assessment of the autobiographical character of Quinto Anfossi, see C. Milanini, *L'utopia discontinua: Saggio su Italo Calvino* (Milan, Garzanti, 1990), pp. 94–95.

[14] G. Pescio-Bottino, *Calvino* (Florence, La nuova Italia, coll. Il Castoro, 1976), p. 70.

one looks at the works from the point of view of the protagonist; though it also seems right to bear in mind that in *La speculazione edilizia* the last hope to which Quinto cannot but turn is in fact still the help of his former party-comrade Masera, who offers him aid as disinterested as it is unexpected. His final rescue indicates that the strength of a progressive ideology and political solidarity might be limited in its wider impact, but is still able to make a difference in small-scale cases.

CHAPTER IV

The Inner Landscape

The works analysed in this chapter were written over a period of nearly thirty years. The different genres to which they belong and the temporal distance between them are such that it would not really make sense to bring them together under any other similarity, were it not for their special treatment of the landscape as an image/symbol.

The various theoretical statements formulated by Calvino tend to repeat one basic concept, namely that his fiction has as its starting point the decodifying of an image/symbol. Thus we know that the child in the trees or the empty armour are the starting points for *Il barone rampante* and *Il cavaliere inesistente*, and it is the development of all the implications that can be linked to them which constitutes the story line of the narrative. Furthermore, as Mengaldo has already noted when talking of the resumption of the theme of the city, from the opening of 'La nuvola di smog' to *Le città invisibili* via the end of *La giornata di uno scrutatore*, it is clear that 'spesso le opere di Calvino nascono per la dilatazione tematica di una cellula generativa precedente' (Mengaldo 1975, p. 416 and also Bonsaver 1995, pp. 180–88).[1] This is certainly the case with the landscape of Sanremo, and the writings brought together in this chapter confirm it.

The landscape of Sanremo as an image/symbol is, however, atypical because it defies a definitive treatment. For example, the image of the child in the tree which appears first in *Il sentiero dei nidi di ragno*, then briefly in 'La formica argentina', and becomes the central element in *Il barone rampante* does not appear in any later work by Calvino. It is as if the author had actually found a proper and final place for it with *Il barone rampante* and did not need concern himself with it any more. The landscape of Sanremo on the other hand, even when it is treated as a central image/symbol (notably in at least two works: 'Dall'opaco' and *Le città invisibili*), is not really dealt with and crops up again in *Se una notte d'inverno un viaggiatore*, and one can only speculate that had the author lived longer it would probably have reappeared in his work.

The autobiographical element disguised in the representation of this landscape, is not an uncommon phenomenon: suffice it to think of authors such as Joyce and Bassani, whose entire work is set in and anchored to their respective home-towns, or of a painter such as Chagall, who included recognizable profiles of Vitebsk in so many of his paintings. In a way

1 Compare P. V. Mengaldo, 'L'arco e le pietre' (on Calvino's *Le città invisibili*), in *La tradizione del novecento* (Milan, Feltrinelli, 1975), pp. 406–26 (p. 416) and G. Bonsaver, *Il mondo scritto: Forme e ideologia nella narrativa di Italo Calvino* (Turin, Tirrenia, 1995), pp. 180–88.

one might also infer that the literary nature of the link between one author and his or her landscape of childhood, by implying a constant reminder and scheme of reference and comparison for one's experience, adds to the difficulty of relinquishing the theme.

The lie of the inner landscape, whether of childhood or adolescence, may be interpreted in different ways, the first of which is the one which defines it as the earliest touchstone for all the landscapes to follow (*I giovani del Po*, *La strada di S. Giovanni*, 'Dall'opaco' and some sections of *Le città invisibili*); or, as previously in Proust, as the root of psychological tendencies laid down by the environment which first influenced the author (*La strada di S. Giovanni*) or again as an absolute image, basic and inexhaustible because it cannot avoid what it does not encompass ('Dall'opaco', 'La spirale'); as a single resolved fragment ('Il conte di Montecristo'); as an introduction to reflections on memory (*Le città invisibili*) and lastly as a furthest limit, an alpha containing the omega of the individual existence (*Se una notte d'inverno un viaggiatore*).

These are the various routes which we shall now follow. Not surprisingly, for this archaeological delving into the inner world we shall use the instruments and terms codified by psychoanalysis. Irrespective of judgements of taste concerning the use or suitability of psychoanalytical analysis in a literary context, neither author nor reader can avoid it, since it remains the most sophisticated and all-inclusive key to the inner world. The reluctance with which Calvino paraded his own private world in public is well-known (and in many respects admirable), but this does not mean that the boundary between these two worlds is not elusive. After all everything is meaningful, and childhood memories, which are among the most private possible, are indistinguishable from the ego.

Moreover, one may conceive of the individual experience as a further reaffirmation of the general rule, as for instance in the section of *Il castello dei destini incrociati* entitled 'Anch'io cerco di dire la mia' where the narrator appropriates the myth of Oedipus explained by the 'gran pastore d'anime e interprete di sogni Sigismondo da Vindobona' (*Romanzi e racconti* II, 593) or one may transfer the emotional charge retained by the past on to the panorama which has been its backdrop.

To conclude this introductory note, one might say that the landscape of Sanremo appears in these pages as a two-sided presence: on the one hand, as the landscape of memory as a figurative and visual element, on the other as a first psychological landscape.

I giovani del Po

From January 1950 until July 1951 Calvino worked on a novel which he published only many years later, in serial form, in a specialist review rather than as an independent book. Indeed, in the introductory note he claims to have published it as material for discussion and analysis. The novel in question, *I giovani del Po* (1957–58), is unfinished, which makes any definitive judgement problematical and unjust. Nonetheless, and within these limits, *I giovani del Po* seems highly relevant for the present analysis.

The novel consists in part of correspondence between two friends, and in part of a third-person narrative. The correspondents are Nino Torre, a worker and trade unionist in an unnamed city (clearly Turin), and his childhood friend Nanin, a general mechanic who has continued to live in a small town on the Riviera. The narrative insertions in the third person, however, concern only the syndicate and amorous activities of Nino Torre in Turin. It is therefore evident that the activity is mainly urban and that Nino is its undisputed protagonist: Nanin does not contribute to the development of the plot in any way, his is an offstage voice with a double role, on the one hand as the exact opposite of Nino and on the other as a figment, a shadow from his past.

The pair represent a contrast between the man of action and the intellectual. While Nino is practical, positive, committed to union organization and interested in debate with his fellows, Nanin appears introverted and bitter, taciturn and pessimistic, unable to find satisfactory solutions to the problems he sees around him. Love for nature, deeply felt by both, is charged with eroticism in Nino's stories and with deeply-felt unhappiness in Nanin's reflections:

> Caro Nino. Puoi fare l'operaio e il sindacalista e il filosofo, non ti dirò mai che non devi farlo, e se lo fai bene ti dirò anche bravo. Però l'unica cosa che non credo buona è che tu parta sempre con illusioni spropositate: arrivare al nocciolo di tutto, trovare la chiave del meccanismo generale. Non c'è né meccanismo né chiave, sta tranquillo. Se arrivi a capire bene una cosa, tutte le altre ti sfuggono e smentiscono quella che capisci. Una cosa è vera solo se serve a qualcos'altra vera allo stesso modo. Tutto quel che facciamo è limitato e misero. Fabbrichiamo motori e fucili e siamo in questo più bravi degli uccelli, dei pesci e dei molluschi. Ma chi ti dice che abbiamo ragione noi? Le patelle che stanno attaccate allo scoglio, e sono rotonde e piatte, e hanno un guscio di silice, e non hanno occhi né bocca, e non formulano pensieri ma solo aderiscono col loro corpo a ventosa e si tengono protette in quel loro duro guscio, chi ti dice che non ne capiscano di più di tutti gli uomini di quel che è successo e succede e può succedere? T'ho detto come la penso io. Ciao. NANIN.
>
> (*Romanzi e racconti* III, 1113)

Here and elsewhere Nanin talks from a non-anthropocentric point of view, as an ascetic naturalist. His dialectical function seems to be to broaden Nino's debate, to set it in a wider context in which humanity, whether in the private sphere or as social interaction, is of little account. But his superior wisdom does not help to make him particularly sympathetic or alive, his epistolatory warnings remain too isolated not to appear incongruous. The decision to imagine the limpets' point of view, too, will reappear in 'La spirale', apparently «la più interessante» of the 'cosmicomic' stories for their author (*Romanzi e racconti* II, 1344). Here, moreover, the narrator is Qfwfq, that is to say a sort of universal narrator who, while using an anthropomorphic language, is not human and has no moral obligation vis-à-vis History. This saves him from the impasse in which Nanin finds himself since, to survive, he cannot avoid taking decisions which go against his ideals:

> Perché l'importante è continuare a avere la propria idea, anche se per una ragione o per l'altra si finisce sempre per fare tutto il contrario. [...] Io invece sono sempre quello di prima anche se faccio cose che avrei giurato di non fare mai; se vuoi saperlo, ho lavorato con l'impresa Groppelli, per conto del Comune, all'impianto delle barche illuminate per la festa padronale.
>
> (*Romanzi e racconti* III, 1050)

Far from being paradisiacal, life in close contact with nature is a continual process of conflict with oneself or with anyone abusing nature, for instance the Town Hall, until one no longer knows which side to be on, whether with men against nature, or vice versa. The dilemma emerges in a letter in which Nanin tells Nino that a mutual acquaintance has lost a hand when fishing with explosives:

> Così Niculin è rovinato; dài e dài l'hanno avuta vinta i pesci. Alle volte penso che sto dalla parte sbagliata, che dovrei tenere per i pesci, i corvi, le formiche. E quando gli uomini hanno il fatto loro, rallegrarmi. Forse il genere umano sta per distruggersi; io al momento buono passerò dall'altra parte: con le formiche o con chiunque verrà. Ma non c'è modo d'uscirne. Chi ama i pesci e gli animali selvatici gli dà la caccia, finché uno distrugge l'altro, come capita. Non c'è altro rapporto che questo farsi a pezzi [...] ci sbraneremo tutti finché ne resterà una fibra. Ma forse ogni cosa si disfa e ricresce.
>
> (*Romanzi e racconti* III, 1095)

The second aspect of Nanin's personality is that he is extraneous to the action. When Nino returns to the Riviera for the holidays, the reader expects an account of some conversations with his friend, but the three letters which mark his arrival, his stay and his return do not make any mention of them:

> Caro Nanin, prepara le lenze, gli ami, i vermi, gli arpioni, le punte per i ricci, i fucili, le maschere, le vele, i remi, cos'altro? La nostra motocicletta se non te la sei venduta, il mio tascapane. Sabato arrivo. Evviva. Nino.
>
> Cara Giovanna, tutto è come l'avevo lasciato: le frane, le pietre, i muri, e la cadenza del mio dialetto, l'alzata di spalle dei miei amici, i gesti che si fa quando si pesca, quando s'innaffia i garofani, il verso della ghiandaia, il sapore della focaccia, degli zucchini ripieni. Ma ora è come se avessi quattro occhi: i due di me che sono cresciuto qui e ho sempre avuto intorno queste cose tutti i giorni della mia vita, e i due di me che sono arrivato da fuori e per cui tutto è nuovo e straordinario. Quattro occhi non sempre dànno una vista completa: spesso ci sento in mezzo il vuoto dei mesi che sono stato via e che intanto sono passati anche qui. Ed ecco quel che devo dirti: se ci fossi tu mi piacerebbe ritrovare i miei posti mostrandoli a te. Ora, per me solo, tutto mi sembra un po' sprecato, anche i ricordi. Nino.
>
> [...]
>
> Caro Nanin, Per te l'estate continua ancora e per me è già finita.
>
> (*Romanzi e racconti* III, 1108–09)

Nanin is conspicuous by his absence. It is as though Calvino intended to develop the character of Nanin at a later date and instead abandoned the manuscript entirely. But, keeping to the text as it stands, it seems rather that Nanin is merely Nino's second pair of eyes; and rather unreliable eyes at that, separated by time.

So why try to bring the Riviera into a story that is mainly about Turin? Perhaps because the Riviera is the starting point for the ethics of civic commitment, the place where the protagonist learned to appreciate what he has around him, and at the same time a term of comparison for the present, as in the contrast between the sea and the Po:

> Nino avrebbe voluto spiegare quel che andava scoprendo: che il fiume è tutto il contrario del mare, che il senso del mare è nell'essere deserto e smisurato: per poco uno s'inoltri non distingue più la gente a riva, va e va e non vede più neanche la terra, e il mare, il mare vero comincia solo allora; il fiume senza nessuno invece è squallido, via per quel principio di pianura; il fiume ha un senso per quel tanto che c'è gente che gli va addosso, che si fa portare da lui, gli fa festa, gli lavora intorno, lo intorbida, lo guasta.
>
> (*Romanzi e racconti* III, 1014)

There is no remotely panoramic description of the Riviera, no glimpse of landscape, but brief references, recognizable details (for instance in Nino's letter to Giovanna quoted above) which aim to depict a way of life in the open air rather than a specific panorama.

Perhaps because they are part of an unfinished work, the landscape of the Riviera and the character of Nanin have in common their remoteness and lack of tangibility; but perhaps only because they belong to memory.

La strada di San Giovanni

I giovani del Po (1950–51) and *La strada di San Giovanni* (1962) are separated by eleven years, during which the landscape of Sanremo appears several times — to mention only *Il visconte dimezzato*, 'La formica argentina', *L'entrata in guerra* and *Il barone rampante* — with the descriptive functions and criteria analysed in the previous chapters. The subject of the story is strictly autobiographical and, indeed, is linked fairly directly with the conclusion of 'Le notti dell'UNPA' in which, as we have seen, the main character, while falling asleep, conjures up the figure of his father, who sets off for the fields at dawn. It is also linked to the shorter 'Uomo nei gerbidi' and in general to the family atmosphere of that narrative section included in *I racconti* under the title 'Le memorie difficili'.

The similarities with these writings cease at the level of content; in that, here too, the main subject of the narrative is the climb up the hill with the narrator's father, along the tracks and pathways leading to the Calvino family holding. But the autobiographical material is now presented from a totally different viewpoint and the ascent of the hill is laden with psychological connotations and existential reflections which could be inferred, but which were not openly expressed, in the earlier stories. Here, for instance, we are told for the first time, that the outing follows a set route to be taken on alternate days like some unpleasant medicine, and that a cluster of guilt mechanism and trials of will links the young writer's steps to those of his father.

This is undoubtedly an attempt at 'sincere' autobiography, which we may infer to be a path every bit as arduous and uncongenial to the author's tastes, if he had duly steered clear of it until this story. We already know that for Calvino there are at least two modes of autobiographical writing, as it can be deduced from the letter to Lucio Mastronardi:

> 'Autobiografarsi' è l'operazione letteraria più difficile, sia se ci si propone l'assoluta verità secondo l'arduo esempio di Rousseau, sia se si sceglie (come fanno i più) una qualche forma di mistificazione (che sarà sempre un modo di dire la verità anche quello).
>
> (*I libri degli altri*, pp. 561–62)

La strada di S. Giovanni is the most outstanding attempt at absolute autobiographical truth. The three stories which make up *L'entrata in guerra* too (if not the whole section entitled 'Le memorie difficili') should be understood as explicitly autobiographical, but the very choice of the stories' content, opportunely limited to isolated episodes and exceptional events, lends itself to a fictionalized rendering rather than to introspective analysis. They should certainly be regarded as so many parts of an autobiography which was never completely written; however, it should be emphasized that *La strada di San Giovanni* is markedly more direct, particularly in terms of its reflections on family matters, which in *L'entrata in guerra* are presented mainly from the outside, almost entirely as relevant sociological data.[2]

[2] Calvino's dislike for any exposure of information on his personal life is well known, well documented, and well publicized. The first monographic study on his work contained one of the briefest biographical notes imaginable: 'Italo Calvino é nato all' Avana nel 1923. Tornato bambino in Italia, ha vissuto a Sanremo finché si é trasferito a Torino nel dopoguerra, lavorando presso la casa editrice Einaudi. Ha viaggiato in Russia e in America ed ora abita a Parigi', G. Pescio-Bottino, *Calvino* (Florence, La nuova Italia, Il Castoro, 1976), p. 3. Moreover it does not contain lies as was threatened in a letter by Calvino to Pescio-Bottino: 'Gentile Signora, sono contento che Lei voglia dedicarmi una monografia. Contento e anche spaventato, perché finora monografie non me ne avevano dedicate e mi credevo in salvo, dato che conto di far dimenticare il mio nome nel giro di pochi anni. [...] Dati biografici: io sono ancora di quelli che credono, con Croce, che di un autore contano solo le opere. (Quando contano, naturalmente). Perciò dati biografici non ne do, o li do falsi, o comunque cerco sempre di cambiarli da una volta all'altra. Mi chieda pure quel che vuol sapere e Glielo dirò. Ma non Le dirò mai la verità, di questo può star sicura', I. Calvino, *I libri degli altri. Lettere 1947–1981*, p. 479. Such a frivolous attitude is more honest than it might seem, since the alteration of data is at the base of Calvino's creative approach. It produces also another divertissment: 'Sono nato nel 1923 sotto un cielo in cui il Sole raggiante e il cupo Saturno erano ospiti dell'armoniosa Bilancia. Passai i primi venticinque anni della mia vita nell'a quei tempi ancor verdeggiante Sanremo, che univa apporti cosmopoliti ed eccentrici alla chiusura scontrosa della sua rustica concretezza; dagli uni e dagli altri aspetti restai segnato per la vita. Poi mi tenne Torino operosa e razionale dove il rischio d'impazzire (come già il Nietzsche) non é minore che altrove. Vi arrivai in anni in cui le strade si aprivano deserte e interminabili per la rarità delle auto. Per abbreviare i miei percorsi di pedone attraversavo le vie rettilinee in lunghe oblique da un angolo all'altro — procedura oggi, oltre che impossibile, impensabile — e così avanzavo tracciando invisibili ipotenuse tra grigi cateti. Sparsamente conobbi altre inclite metropoli, atlantiche e pacifiche, di tutte innamorandomi a prima vista, d'alcune illudendomi d'averle comprese e possedute, altre restandomi inafferabili e straniere. Per lunghi anni soffersi di una nevrosi geografica: non riuscivo a stare tre giorni di seguito in nessuna città o luogo. Alla fine elessi stabilmente sposa e dimora a Parigi, città circondata da foreste di faggi e carpini e betulle, in cui passeggio con mia figlia Abigail, e circondante a sua volta la *Bibliothèque Nationale*, dove mi reco a consultare testi rari, usufruendo della *Carte de Lecteur* n. 2516. Così, preparato al Peggio, sempre più incontentabile riguardo al Meglio, già pregusto le gioie incomparabili dell'invecchiare' (*Saggi* II, 2770–71). In the quotation above the name of his daughter has the ring of an academic joke, and anyhow it is false; the hint to astrology which seems here completly ironic turns out to be genuine elsewhere, see *Saggi* I, 675–76; and finally the image of an anonymous reader of the *Bibliothèque Nationale* is one in line with the information later contained in *Eremita a Parigi.* The reference to Croce in the letter quoted above helps to understand the pose of philosophical detachment from fame and publicity. It is very interesting to note however that as for the

It should be noted that according to Lejeune's classification, only this story respects what he calls the 'autobiographical pact', in that only here, and however obliquely, does the author's surname appear, and one may thus be certain that it is indeed an autobiography (Lejeune 1975, pp. 13–46 and also Milanini, pp. 91–96),[3] while for 'Le memorie difficili' one may talk only of a recurrence of autobiographical elements, or of ambiguous autobiography because neither the title, nor the stories themselves ever give evidence of any definite correspondence between the author and the narrating 'I'. Here, on the contrary, the account of his climbs with his father is distinctly personal. The story, treated as an extremely detailed recollection, opens with an anti-climax:

> Una spiegazione generale del mondo e della storia deve innanzi tutto tenere conto di com'era situata casa nostra
>
> (*Romanzi e racconti* III, 7)

whose comic intent may be interpreted as a send-up of the biographer's sense of self-importance, and as reflecting the candour of an assertion formulated according to the reductive parameters of infantile thought. The first-person narrator who in 'Uomo nei gerbidi' was presented with individual characteristics which would cut him off from others by virtue of his superior imagination, though without any excessive complacency, bore traces of a romantic individualism completely foreign to this story.[4] Here, right from the start, individualism is a given fact, basic and indispensable, which can be explained and described in spatial terms, because, according to the infantile topography on which the story is based, the world stands to the one side of the house, and history to the other. We may understand the former as the world of the father, which clearly represents the relation with nature, and the latter as that of the 'city', chosen by the first-person narrator as the representation of history. Although this topographical symbolic system is already apparent in 'Uomo nei gerbidi', it should be stressed yet again that what was only implicit in the 1946 story is here made patent.

The purpose of the first-person narrator is undoubtedly to celebrate the past through the greatest possible truthfulness to life: here this takes the form of a list of proper names, which, as the narrator himself admits, have long fallen into disuse. Thus we learn at the outset that the region in question was called 'Punta di Francia' and that San Giovanni is the place where the author's father had his model holding. This archaeological fervour is explained in one of the numerous parentheses in the passage:

> (i nomi, ora che le cose non esistono più, si impongono insostituibili e perentori sulla pagina per essere salvati)
>
> (*Romanzi e racconti* III, 8)

---

autobiographical quality of his writing, his attitude shifted in time, see for example C. Milanini, *L'utopia discontinua: Saggio su Italo Calvino* (Milan, Garzanti, 1990), p. 92 and that gradually Calvino became slightly more open, see especially 'Situazione 1978', and 'Intervista di Maria Corti', both in *Saggi* II, 2828–34 and 2920–29.

3 P. Lejeune, *Le Pacte autobiographique* (Paris, Editions du Seuil, 1975), pp. 13–46 and C. Milanini, *L'utopia discontinua: Saggio su Italo Calvino* (Milan, Garzanti, 1990), pp. 91–96.

4 This applies above all to the narrator's considerations on Corsica, see *Romanzi e racconti* I, 186.

Yet even if we allow that these names do retain the emotive charge that the author seems to attribute to them, as indicators of signs and spatial confines in the local idiolect of a vanished community, we are somehow led to suspect that they are chiefly important because they were not so before, and that they appear as a form of amends; just like the Latin names of the various species of plants which the author refused to learn as a boy, and which he invents at the moment of writing, creating a kind of parodic onomastics which is the most successful part of the story.

Both the names of places and the names of plants are indissolubly linked to the figure of the father:

> Per mio padre i nomi dovevano servire da conferma alle cose e da segno di possesso; per me erano previsioni di cose intraviste appena, non possedute, presunte. Il vocabolario di mio padre si dilatava nell'interminabile catalogo dei generi, delle specie, delle varietà del regno vegetale — ogni nome era una differenza colta nella densa compattezza della foresta, la fiducia d'avere così allargato il dominio dell'uomo — e nella terminologia tecnica, dove l'esattezza della parola accompagna lo sforzo d'esattezza dell'operazione, del gesto. E tutta questa nomenclatura babelica s'impastava a un fondo idiomatico altrettanto babelico, cui concorrevano diverse lingue, mescolate secondo i bisogni e i ricordi, (il dialetto per le cose locali e brusche — aveva un lessico dialettale di ricchezza rara, pieno di voci cadute in disuso —, lo spagnolo per le cose generali e gentili — il Messico era stato lo scenario dei suoi anni più fortunati — l'italiano per la retorica — era, in tutto, uomo dell'Ottocento —, l'inglese — aveva visitato il Texas — per la pratica, il francese per lo scherzo) e ne veniva un discorso tessuto d'intercalari che tornavano puntualmente in risposta a situazioni fisse, esorcizzando i moti dell'animo, un catalogo anch'esso, parallelo a quello della nomenclatura agricola, — e a quell'altro non di parole ma di zufolii, pispoli, trilli, zirli, chiù che era dato dalla sua bravura a imitare i versi degli uccelli, sia col semplice atteggiare delle labbra, sia aiutandosi con le mani disposte in modo adatto intorno alla bocca, sia mediante fischietti e macchinette, a fiato o a molla, di cui portava nella cacciatora un vasto assortimento.
>
> (*Romanzi e racconti* III, 11–12)[5]

The above quotation confirms that Calvino is indeed paying homage to his father in these pages, to the point of describing him implicitly as the model for the character of Cosimo, with words which might be taken from a page of *Il barone rampante*:

> e in questo nominare le piante metteva la passione di dar fondo a un universo senza fine, di spingersi ogni volta alle frontiere estreme d'una <u>genealogia</u> vegetale, e da ogni ramo o foglia o nervatura aprirsi una via come fluviale, nella linfa, nella rete che copre la verde terra.
>
> (*Romanzi e racconti* III, 9)[6]

5 Claudio Milanini links the composition of this text in January 1962, to the feeling of loss and mourning on the tenth anniversary of his father's death, see I. Calvino, *Romanzi e racconti* III, 1204. Milanini's interpretation is substantiated by Calvino's letter to Adriana Monti in I. Calvino, *I libri degli altri. Lettere 1947–1981*, p. 379.

6 I have underlined the word 'genealogy' because I believe that it represents a reference both to the title of the trilogy *I nostri antenati* and to the family pride, unshared by Cosimo, of his baron father.

Such a celebration of the father, and at the same time of Calvino's distance from him, of the unbridgeable divide between their two characters, where the silent walk taken along the crest of the hills also represents a mutual hardening of positions; to the point that literature, too, as laborious as the paternal climb, represents that same road to San Giovanni, where San Giovanni stands for the optimal relationship between the author and nature.

> E io? Io credevo di pensare ad altro. Cos'era la natura? Erbe, piante, luoghi verdi, animali. Ci vivevo in mezzo e volevo essere altrove. Di fronte alla natura restavo indifferente, riservato, a tratti ostile. E non sapevo che stavo anch'io cercando un rapporto, forse più fortunato di quello di mio padre, un rapporto che sarebbe stata la letteratura a darmi, restituendo significato a tutto, e d'un tratto ogni cosa sarebbe divenuta vera e tangibile e possedibile e perfetta, ogni cosa di quel mondo ormai perduto.
>
> (*Romanzi e racconti* III, 25)

This reads almost like a résumé of *La Recherche*, except that Calvino's narrator, unlike Proust, is not content with what literature has given him in exchange for the irreparable loss which has given rise to it. Along with his father and the landscape, the past too is lost: memory can capture only its most exhausting aspect, that of the road to San Giovanni itself.

This discontent is linked to a difference of aims: in this story the landscape is not just recollected, the narrative actually takes the form of a self-analysis, in which the first-person narrator considers and treats memory as 'screen memory' (*Deckerinnerung*).[7]

In the layerings of memory, the recollection of the landscape seen along the road to San Giovanni is apparently innocent, but it conceals an unresolved infantile and juvenile hostility towards the father. What the first-person narrator gradually reveals through a juxtaposition of contrasting interpretations contained within parentheses is therefore remorse, relating both to paternal expectations and to his own losses:

> Mentre continuavo a seguire in silenzio mio padre, che additava certe foglie di là da un muro e diceva: 'Ypotoglaxia jasminifolia' (ora invento dei nomi; quelli veri non li ho mai imparati), 'Photophila wolfoides' diceva (sto inventando; erano nomi di questo genere), oppure 'Crotodendron indica' (certo adesso avrei potuto magari cercare dei nomi veri, invece di inventarli, magari riscoprire quali erano in realtà le piante che mio padre andava nominandomi; ma sarebbe stato barare al gioco, non accettare la perdita che mi sono io stesso inflitto, le mille perdite che ci infliggiamo e

7 'Screen memory. = A childhood memory characterised both by its unusual sharpness and by the apparent insignificance of its content. The analysis of such memory leads back to indelible childhood experiences and to unconscious fantasies. Like the symptom, the screen memory is a formation produced by a compromise between repressed elements and defence', in J. Laplanche and J. B. Pontalis, *The Language of Psycho-analysis*, (London, The Hogarth Press, 1973), pp. 410–11. The examples used by Freud to explain the concept of screen memory refer to isolated events, linked to infancy only, while it might be objected that the story consists of a layering of events over time, and goes well over the limits of infancy. But on the one hand this very layering of memories has the function, in the story, of marking a repeated parallel between the arduousness of the father's work and that of writing, to arrive at a partial justification of the first-person narrator, who recovers this very relationship with the natural world through writing. On the other hand in this case it is the repetitiveness of the walks which makes their memory banal, thus acting as a screen to the real memory, which is of the futile city and beach life left at the margin of the story.

> per cui non c'è rivincita). (Eppure, eppure, se avessi scritto qui dei veri nomi di piante sarebbe stato da parte mia un atto di modestia e pietà, finalmente un fare ricorso a quell'umile sapienza che la mia gioventù rifiutava per puntare su carte ignote e infide, sarebbe stato un gesto di pacificazione col padre, una prova di maturità, e invece non l'ho fatto, mi sono compiaciuto di questo scherzo dei nomi inventati, di quest'intenzione di parodia, segno che ancora una resistenza è rimasta, una polemica, segno che la marcia mattutina verso San Giovanni continua ancora, con il suo dissidio, che ogni mattina della mia vita è ancora la mattina in cui tocca a me accompagnare nostro padre a San Giovanni).
>
> (*Romanzi e racconti* III, 12)

Calvino's use of parentheses as found in this story, but also in *La speculazione edilizia* and *La giornata di uno scrutatore,* is the reverse of the norm in Italian prose.[8] Here the parentheses graphically underline the shift from story to information and its interpretation, and are used as so many interruptions to the narrative flow, but they are far from all having the same function. If the first two are surely an ironic wink directed at the reader, from the third onwards the direction of communication is above all between the person who writes and the person who is rereading the text, in a crescendo of complexity. The last sentence of the quotation contains both the word 'resistenza', a technical term from classic psychoanalysis (resistance = Widerstand), and the phrase 'pacificazione col padre', which sounds distinctly Lacanian (coined on the basis of the phrase *symbolic father* or the *Name-of-the-Father*), to alert us to the fact that at this point the first-person narrator is overtly acting as his own analyst.[9]

The interpretation of screen memories is that of bringing to light the infantile desire which they conceal:

> More like a dream than like a piece of documentary evidence, the screen-memory is a disguised representation of unconscious desire. And because in this account, memory is of desire, and desire is forbidden, the most vivid element in an ordinary memory may be the least revealing.
>
> (Phillips 1995, p. 66)[10]

Seen in relation to the seriousness of the remorse of the (adult) first-person narrator, the infantile and juvenile desire which these memories conceal, and which the story just barely reveals in its conclusion, appears all the more futile:

> Vorrei che fossero pronte subito le ceste, per tornare a casa e andare al mare. Il mare è lì, in uno spacco triangolare della valle, a vu; ma è come se fosse miglia e miglia

8 See the animated comment by Alberto Arbasino: 'Ma la più singolare caratteristica esterna-interna della *Giornata di uno scrutatore* sembra il predominio di quella inquietante cifra stilistico-tipografico-psicologica che sono le parentesi: già definite "elementi ritardanti" dopo un famoso saggio di Spitzer (e segno di complicazione, cautela, difficoltà nei rapporti con la vita), e impiegate qui invece a connettere la testimonianza con la riflessione...' (*Saggi* II, 2761).

9 For an explanation of these concepts see J. Laplanche and J. B. Pontalis, *The Language of Psycho-analysis* (London, The Hogarth Press, 1973), especially pp. 394–97, and pp. 439–41.

10 A. Phillips, 'The Telling of Selves', in *On Flirtation* (London, Faber, 1995), p. 66.

> lontano, il mare estraneo a mio padre e a tutta la gente che si muove per le nostre strade mattutine. Ora stiamo tornando. Io cammino curvo sotto la mia gerla. Il sole è alto; dalla carrozzabile più vicina, sulla collina di San Giacomo, romba un camion; qui nella valle il grigio degli olivi e il fruscio del torrente smorzano i colori e i suoni. Sull'altro versante sale dalla terra un fumo: qualcuno ha acceso un debbio. Mio padre dice qualcosa sulla mignolatura degli olivi. Io non ascolto. Guardo il mare e penso che tra un'ora sarò alla spiaggia. Alla spiaggia le ragazze lanciano palloni con le braccia lisce, si tuffano nel luccichio, gridano, schizzano, su tanti sandolini e pedalò.
>
> (*Romanzi e racconti* III, 26)

The conclusion is cleverly multifaceted, and I shall note only the most striking of the possible interpretations. As a sincere analysis of memory (and as a text that is in some sense private), it bears witness to an awareness of loss of a relationship with the father and of the culture the father represents. Yet the recollection is not strictly for private use, and to consider the story as self-analysis pure and simple would be mistaken: the information and apostrophes to the reader are so numerous that the intimate and confessional aspect of the recollection is undoubtedly exorcised. The narrator's flirtation with an audience of addressees implied in the text guarantees its transformation from private memory to autobiography, from introspection to story, with the conventional characteristics typical of the genre, and those to which Calvino in particular has accustomed us. Thus from recollection to recollection, from emotional reconstruction to intellectual reconstruction, constantly raising the stakes and making the route increasingly problematic, the first-person narrator has had us climb the road to San Giovanni, revealing to us only at the end that his real life lies elsewhere, and that he is not going to talk about it anyway.[11]

'La spirale'

The impasse of which Nanin is a victim does not find a solution in *I giovani del Po*, but is is interesting to note that the above-quoted passage in which he tries to see the world through the eyes of the limpets gives rise to a far more successful text, namely 'La spirale' (1965). Among the series of *Le Cosmicomiche*, 'La spirale' marks a very clear departure in Calvino's fiction: it is the beginning of a way of narrating which no longer sets out to represent human events naturalistically, but in a coded and symbolic fashion, like a mathematical expression.

[11] Both the opening and the ending of *La strada di San Giovanni* are highly literary: in the unfinished section of *Lezioni americane* titled 'Cominciare e finire', Calvino analyses famous beginnings and endings in world literature and concludes that: 'Comunque, inizio e finale, anche se possiamo considerarli simmetrici sul piano teorico, non lo sono sul piano estetico. La storia della letteratura è ricca d'incipit memorabili, mentre i finali che presentino una vera originalità come forma e come significato sono più rari, o almeno non si presentano alla memoria così facilmente' (*Saggi* I, 750–51). Even more relevant for my purpose is the following consideration on endings: 'Il problema di non finire una storia è questo. Comunque essa finisca, qualsiasi sia il momento in cui una storia può considerarsi finita, ci accorgiamo che non è verso quel punto che portava l'azione del raccontare, che quello che conta è altrove, è ciò che è avvenuto prima: è il senso che acquista quel segmento isolato di accadimenti, estratto dalla continuità del raccontabile. [...] Il finale veramente importante è quello che come nell'*Education sentimentale* mette in discussione tutta la narrazione, la gerarchia di valori che presiede il romanzo' (*Saggi* I, 748–49).

What interests us, however, is to note how, as a text, 'La spirale' differs from the other stories in *Le Cosmicomiche* in that, unlike the others, it is not introduced by a short section putting forward a scientific theory, but by a simple authorial reflection:

> *Per la maggioranza dei molluschi, la forma organica visibile non ha molta importanza nella vita dei membri d'una specie, dato che essi non possono vedersi l'un l'altro o hanno solo una vaga percezione degli altri individui e dell'ambiente. Ciò non esclude che striature a colori vivaci e forme che appaiono bellissime al nostro sguardo (come in molte conchiglie di gasteropodi) esistano indipendentemente da ogni rapporto con la visibilità.*
>
> (*Romanzi e racconti* II, 207)

This decision not to put forward a scientific theory could be considered to underline the metaphorical tone of the narrative — here Calvino could simply have reversed a statement taken from the quantum theory, on how the observer's very presence conditions the phenomenon under examination. Furthermore, the story is divided into three parts; the second of these, differentiated by the use of italics, is the one which will concern us most because it reconstructs the landscape of Sanremo. But before considering this latest appearance of the landscape, we should dwell briefly on the meaning and implications of the text of 'La spirale' as a whole.

Qfwfq's discourse tries to prove a paradoxical theory, that is, that sight depends more upon the images than upon the eyes which will receive them:

> Ora è ridicolo pensare che uno avendo l'encefalo ne dirami un nervo come fosse una lenza tirata al buio e finché non gli spuntano gli occhi non possa sapere se fuori c'è qualcosa da vedere o no. Io di questo materiale non avevo niente, quindi ero il meno autorizzato a parlarne; però mi ero fatto una mia idea e cioè che l'importante era costituire delle immagini visuali, e poi gli occhi sarebbero venuti di conseguenza.
>
> (*Romanzi e racconti* II, 218)

At face value the theory is somewhat absurd; but if, as seems necessary, we replace the faculty of sight with the capacity to criticize and enjoy the world or, basically, to 'see' it, it becomes clear that the shell of which Qfwfq is speaking represents art, that is literature, music and everything we call creative.[12] Qfwfq's approach is also a reflection of the

12 That the verb 'vedere' is used in a broad sense is obvious and requires no further comment; interestingly, Anna Dolfi suggested that the posthumous collection *Sotto in sole giaguaro* (1986) inspired by the five senses, was to have contained a sixth one roughly definable as 'senso culturale' in A. Dolfi, 'Calvino, l'alfabeto e la morte' in *La Gazzetta di Parma*, 19 June 1987, p. 3. This suggestion is not confirmed by Claudio Milanini's note; on the other hand, from Calvino's annotations for the short story about sight, it is implied that he intended to rework autobiographical material: '30.11. 84 — racconto della vista — partendo dalla ricerca dei funghi col padre, riflettendo sull'«intenzione del fungo»: nascondersi? ma la sua forma è anche visiva: farsi vedere? Il mondo come oggetto visivo. Gli occhi, i nostri occhi come strumento attraverso cui il mondo si vede. Quanto abbiamo visto? = quanto abbiamo aiutato il mondo — le cose, le persone a vedersi, cioè a esserci? Arte: crea visività (ornamenti, forma oggetti, astrattismo) e trasmette visività (pittura 'dal vero', pittura 'sulla' vista cioè impressionismo). (E la fotograf.? il cine?) Le cose rimaste al margine del campo visivo. E le persone? I segni che uno trasmette (anche ai ciechi). I segni nascosti sono da cercare, come i funghi. Il mondo non è un panopticon ma un pancripticon. Non il nascosto occulto (viscere, segreto) ma il nascosto con intenzione d'essere trovato (tracce, tesoro nascosto)' (*Romanzi e racconti* III, 1214–15).

reiterated authorial claim that his writing starts with an image-symbol.[13] The whole story should be understood as a metaphor for artistic creation, from its obscure gestation, partly spontaneous, partly the fruit of an intentional act of self-differentiation, down to the final product:

> questa conchiglia era una cosa diversa da me ma anche la parte più vera di me, la spiegazione di chi ero io, il mio ritratto tradotto in un sistema ritmico di volumi e strisce e colori e roba dura
>
> (*Romanzi e racconti* II, 213)

The metaphor is so explicit that we shall not insist on this point except to say that this would inevitably have to be the instrument, or possibly the device, offering a way out of the trap into which Nanin's philosophizing had fallen.[14]

The second section of the story, differentiated by the use of italics, marks a qualitative shift in the characterization of the narrator; here Qfwfq is no longer a mollusc and, although there is no indication of the species to which he belongs, it is certainly one endowed with sight.

> *(Tanto che adesso, passati cinquecento milioni d'anni, mi guardo intorno e vedo*
>
> (*Romanzi e racconti* II, 214)

What Qfwfq sees is the bay of Sanremo, but the perspective is reversed: rather than from the top of the hill, the visual angle starts from the rock with the limpets, and zigzags upwards.

> *vedo sopra lo scoglio la scarpata ferroviaria e il treno che ci passa sopra* [...] *e sparisce nella galleria sopra alla quale corre la strada camionale con il cartellone «Volate Egyptair» che rappresenta le piramidi, e un motofurgoncino di gelati tenta di sorpassare un camion* [...] *ma poi frena e si riaccoda perché la visibilità è impedita da una nuvola di api che attraversa la strada proveniente da una fila di alveari situati in un campo da cui certamente un'ape regina sta volando via tirandosi dietro tutto uno sciame in senso contrario al fumo del treno rispuntato all'altra estremità della galleria, cosicché non si vede più nulla per questo strato nuvoloso di api e fumo di carbone, se non alcuni metri più sopra un contadino che rompe la terre a colpi di zappa* [...] *in un orto che circonda un osservatorio astronomico con i telescopi puntati al cielo*
>
> (*Romanzi e racconti* II, 214–15)

The observatory (a real one which still exists in Sanremo and belonged to the author's father) is required by the story: at this moment Qfwfq is interested in a vision which includes human activity in history, as the references to Herodotus, the pyramids, the chance finding of a fragment of neolithic hoe, the shape of the Zodiac of Chaldean astronomers and so on show, and the observatory serves as a reference to the measurement of time.

13 See p. 67 above, Postfazione ai *Nostri antenati* (*Romanzi e racconti* I, 1210) and *Lezioni americane* (*Saggi* I, 677 and 696–714).

14 Calvino himself quoted Leopardi as among the sources of inspiration for *Le Cosmicomiche*; and it seems to me that in his repertoire of symbolic images, the limpets correspond to Leopardi's 'ginestra'. See also G. Bonsaver, *Il mondo scritto: Forme e ideologia nella narrativa di Italo Calvino* (Turin, Tirrenia, 1995), p. 96.

In relation to the previous descriptions of the Ligurian landscape, the perspective is reversed because it is narrated by an anti-character, a character far removed from any traditional role, above all by its reluctance to take on human form. This detachment from human representation is highly provocative, not only because it offers continual comic opportunities but because it does not allow us to pause on the negative aspects inherent in every specific condition, including that of the '*fuchi che agonizzano in fondo all'alveare dopo aver compiuto il loro atto di continuazione della specie*' (*Romanzi e racconti* II, 217).

Even in the final section, a gasteropod once again, Qfwfq does not complain much of being without eyes, indeed he boasts of having made them possible:

> Tutti questi occhi erano miei. Li avevo resi possibili io; io avevo avuto la parte attiva; io gli fornivo la materia prima, l'immagine. Con gli occhi era venuto tutto il resto, quindi tutto ciò che gli altri, avendo gli occhi, erano diventati, in ogni loro forma e funzione, e la quantità di cose che avendo gli occhi erano riusciti a fare, in ogni loro forma e funzione, veniva fuori da quel che avevo fatto io. Non per nulla erano implicite nel mio star lì, nel mio aver relazioni con gli altri e con le altre eccetera, nel mio mettermi a fare la conchiglia eccetera. Insomma avevo previsto proprio tutto.
>
> (*Romanzi e racconti* II, 220–21)

The irony of the last sentence stems from by the pomposity that characterizes the narrator, and it is the final comic touch, because he immediately concludes with a further stylistic switch:

> E in fondo a ognuno di quegli occhi abitavo io, ossia abitava un altro me, una delle immagini di me, e s'incontrava con l'immagine di lei, nell'ultramondo che s'apre attraversando la sfera semiliquida delle iridi, il buio delle pupille, il palazzo degli specchi delle rètine, nel vero nostro elemento che si estende senza rive né confini.
>
> (*Romanzi e racconti* II, 221)

The story's moral is certainly not simplistic; on the other hand it is understandable that, like all attempts at the overall integration of nature, history and humanity, it too should generate suspicion, as we immediately see, to quote Calvino himself: 'Così ho messo tutto a posto. Sulla pagina almeno. Dentro di me tutto resta come prima' (*Romanzi e racconti* II, 602). The page in question also marks the appearance of a deeper and more enduring dimension, a consoling dimension which had always been present but which the author had never previously explicitly explored. One might compare this ending with that of 'La formica argentina' (quoted above, p. 57) where we find that the allusion is the same: in both cases the 'happy ending' comes from the universal communion of elements, but while the narrator of 'La formica argentina' presents his thinking in the form of an intuition and momentary sense of relief which also marks the end of the story, Qfwfq talks with complete assurance throughout. Two reasons come to mind to explain this change. The first is that the sense of the adventurous and the novelistic were less and less interesting to Calvino: the instinctive liveliness of the young narrator who feels his own historical responsibility as a moral and didactic task is replaced by the hesitancy of a narrator who no longer has any great certainties upon which to build his discourse.[15] The sense of bereavement, of rarefaction, of uncertainty in the mature Calvino (the Calvino who offers the most explicit and painful self-portrait in *La giornata di uno scrutatore*), has raised many doubts and much resistance among critics. First among them Calvino himself, who long tried to resist the feared spectre of the 'mare dell'oggettività' maintaining his own unilinear voluntarism for as long as he could, expressed paradigmatically in the assertion in Postfazione ai *Nostri antenati*:

> una persona si pone volontariamente una difficile regola e la segue fino alle sue ultime conseguenze, perché senza di questa non sarebbe se stesso né per sé né per gli altri.
>
> (*Romanzi e racconti* I, 1213)

The rule, from Qfwfq onwards, is to narrate the narratable, abandoning any play of predictions, any attempt at constituting a position of reference for generations to come. Thus Orlando, in *Il castello dei destini incrociati*, is transformed from a paladin of action into a contemplative ascetic and refuses to go back to being as he was before.

> Voleva dire che comunque giri poi viene il momento che lo acchiappano e lo legano, Orlando, e gli ricacciano in gola l'intelletto rifiutato?
>
> Nell'ultima carta si contempla il paladino legato a testa in giù come L'Appeso. E finalmente ecco il suo viso diventato sereno e luminoso, l'occhio limpido come neppure nell'esercizio delle sue ragioni passate. Cosa dice? Dice: — Lasciatemi così. Ho fatto tutto il giro e ho capito. Il mondo si legge all'incontrario. Tutto è chiaro.
>
> (*Romanzi e racconti* II, 532)

'Il conte di Montecristo'

The theme of the spiral as a concentric fortress which grows upon itself returns in 'Il conte di Montecristo' (*Romanzi e racconti* II, 344–56), written in 1967. Edmond Dantès, the

[15] See *Palomar*, in *Romanzi e racconti* II, 961–63. From the following, and much quoted section of 'Il midollo del leone': 'Noi pure siamo tra quelli che credono in una letteratura che sia presenza attiva nella storia, in una letteratura come educazione, di grado e di qualità insostituibile. [...] Le cose che la letteratura può ricercare e insegnare sono poche ma insostituibili: il modo di guardare il prossimo e se stessi, di porre in relazione fatti personali e fatti generale, di attribuire valore a piccole cose o a grandi, di considerare i propri limiti e vizi e gli altrui, di trovare le proporzioni della vita, e il posto dell'amore in essa, e la sua forza e il suo ritmo, e il posto della morte e il pensarci o non pensarci; la letteratura può insegnare la durezza, la pietà, la tristezza, l'ironia, l'umorismo e tante altre cose necessarie e difficili. Il resto lo si vada a imparare altrove, dalla scienza, dalla storia, dalla vita, come noi tutti dobbiamo continuamente andare a impararlo' (*Saggi* I, 21–22). To the foreword to *Lezioni americane*: 'La mia fiducia nel futuro della letteratura consiste nel sapere che ci sono cose che solo la letteratura può dare coi suoi mezzi specifici. Vorrei duque dedicare queste conferenze ad alcuni valori o qualità o specificità della letteratura che mi stanno particolarmente a cuore, cercando di situarle nella prospettiva del nuovo millennio' (*Saggi* I, 629). It may be noted that there is a fundamental unity and consistency in Calvino's professions of faith in literature. What has certainly disappeared is the optimistic and somewhat boastful tone. The former spells out and emphasizes a list of practical purposes in literature. It is a list tinged with post-war, left-wing, optimistic positivism. In *Lezioni americane* the emphasis is on a degree of conciseness which could be called elliptic and on the individual taste (rather than the common good). See also A. Berardinelli, 'Calvino moralista: ovvero, restare sani dopo la fine del mondo' Diario, 9 (February 1991), 37–58 (p. 52), G. C. Ferretti, *Le capre di Bikini — Calvino giornalista e saggista 1945–1985* (Roma, Editori Riuniti, 1989), pp. 154–59, and C. Milanini, *L'utopia discontinua: Saggio su Italo Calvino* (Milan, Garzanti, 1990), pp. 164–67 and pp. 184–87.

narrator of the last of the 'cosmicomic' stories contained in *Ti con zero*, has been locked for years in a cell in the fortress of If. He has lost his sense of direction, from within the prison he can see a rectangle of empty sky and hear the sound of the sea:

> La finestrella a grata è in fondo a un cunicolo che fora lo spessore del muro: non inquadra nessuna vista; dalla luminosità più o meno intensa del cielo riconosco pressapoco le ore e le stagioni; ma non so se sotto s'apra il mare o gli spalti o uno dei cortili interni della fortezza. [...] Il mare lo si sente battere, specie le notti di tempesta: alle volte pare quasi che le onde si rompano qui contro la parete alla quale accosto l'orecchio; alle volte pare scavino dal basso, sotto gli scogli delle fondamenta, e la mia cella sia in cima alla torre più alta, e il rombo salga per la prigione, anch'esso prigioniero, come nella tromba di una conchiglia.
>
> (*Romanzi e racconti* II, 344–45)

This irretrievable loss of any sense of direction dooms all attempts at escape by the old Abate Faria, who no longer distinguishes even the zenith from the nadir:

> Alle volte sento grattare il soffitto; cade una pioggia di calcinacci; s'apre una breccia; ne spunta la testa di Faria capovolta. Capovolta per me, non per lui; striscia fuori della sua galleria, cammina a testa in giù senza che nulla si scomponga nella sua persona: né i capelli bianchi, né la barba verde di muffa, né i brandelli di tela di sacco che ricoprono i suoi lombi macilenti. Percorre come una mosca il soffitto e le pareti; si ferma, conficca il piccone in un punto, s'apre un pertugio; scompare.
>
> (*Romanzi e racconti* II, 347)

If Dantès is the narrator, Faria is the character. If both are fictitious, Faria is so in a different way from Dantès (for instance, he is not subject to the law of gravity, whereas 'i calcinacci' still are). If Faria is a man of action and proceeds pragmatically, overcoming one obstacle at a time, Dantès is the theoretician who comments, unfavourably, upon his general behaviour:

> ma nel momento in cui l'ultimo colpo di piccone dovrebbe aprirgli il varco sulla scogliera, s'accorge d'essere sbucato in una cella ancora più interna di quella da cui era partito. Basta un piccolo errore nei calcoli, un lieve scarto nell'inclinazione della galleria ed egli s'inoltra nelle viscere della fortezza senza più modo di ritrovare la rotta.
>
> (*Romanzi e racconti* II, 345)

While Faria's movements 'continuano ad avvolgersi su se stessi come in un gomitolo' (*Romanzi e racconti* II, 347), Dantès decides that he can think of escape only by choosing Faria as protagonist. For Dantès the outside world does not equal freedom, but the past: the pile of sheets of paper ready and waiting to go from Dumas' desk to the printers, a pile of paper which

> contiene la Marsiglia della mia giovinezza; percorrendo le righe di fitta scrittura posso farmi largo sui moli del porto, risalire la Rue de la Canèbiere nel sole del mattino, raggiungere il villaggio dei Catalani inerpicato sulla collina, rivedere Mercedes...
>
> (*Romanzi e racconti* II, 354)

Return to the past would be counterproductive:

> Se la prigione è circondata dal mio fuori, quel fuori mi riporterebbe dentro ogni volta che riuscissi a raggiungerlo: il fuori non è altro che il passato, è inutile tentare di fuggire.
>
> (*Romanzi e racconti* II, 351)

Thus the route should be reversed,

> Se fuori c'è il passato, forse il futuro si concentra nel punto più interno dell'isola d'If, cioè la via d'uscita è una via verso il dentro.
>
> (*Romanzi e racconti* II, 351)

The inner dimension is a map which is superimposed upon other maps, every line may be followed in different directions, the desire which drives Faria to escape from the prison-fortress has its centripetal reverse in the search for the treasure at the centre of the island of Montecristo. His individual course is predetermined, or at least it is part of the magnetic field of nineteenth-century European history, and his destiny follows that of Napoleon with his escape from the island of Elba, which ends with further imprisonment on St Helena. But Faria cannot yet foresee this and his task is to try to fit the map of his own action into that of the events of the Napoleonic Era. Success does not depend upon his efficiency, but upon the decisions of Dumas, who, moreover, gets help from two collaborators who exhauste all the possible outcomes of each episode. The work cannot include them all, but it will attempt to salvage the most significant combinations, increasing in volume in proportion with the links which are necessary to splice together the best bits.

Just as in the succinct description of the Marseille of 'mia giovinezza' we recognize the essential features of Sanremo (which serves to justify its inclusion here), so in the description of the genesis of the work we get a glimpse of Calvino's narrative method, with the branching of the alternatives thought up by Maquet and Fiorentino in place of the binarism and self-imposed following of an inner rule to its extreme consequences, and with the systolic phase in which Dumas 'sceglie, scarta, ritaglia, incolla, interseca' (*Romanzi e racconti* II, 354). But it is a partial description in that it seems to start from the premise of the existence of the end product, just as Faria digs in the belief that the fortress does hold a way which leads to escape.

Dantès, on the other hand, although aware that his destiny lies, already written, among the variants strewing Dumas' desk, and that in one of them, that which earlier on he would have preferred, his innocence and vengeance triumph over his persecutors, remains indifferent to this particular solution, and looks for a way out of his prison among the rejected material, that is, the hypothetical point of contact between the reality of the 'fuori' and the principles of the 'dentro'.

Considering Dantès as the mouthpiece for Calvino's attitude to literature, one would reach the conclusion in the opinion of Francesca Bernardini that:

> compito della letteratura allora non è tanto quello di indicare una via d'uscita dalla prigione-labirinto, quanto un metodo, ed in sede ideologica di garantire la possibilità di un mondo autre, di cui il libro è sempre per metafora un progetto.
>
> (Bernardini 1977, p. 57)[16]

[16] F. Bernardini, *I segni nuovi di Italo Calvino* (Roma, Bulzoni, 1977), p. 57.

The explanation is very satisfactory from the theoretical point of view. The dark nature of the representational choice, on the other hand, becomes clearer if one adopts a psychological approach, according to which Dantès dilemma is that of an ego rebelling against the edifying decisions of the super-ego-Dumas, and against the narrowness of the instinctive id-Faria. The result is a fragmentation by which the ego, rather than refined, is gradually weakened, to the point of becoming reduced to the paralysed awareness of the later figure of Palomar.[17]

'Dall'opaco'

Observing the chronology of publication dates because of lack of reliable information concerning their real order of composition, the text in which the Sanremo landscape next appears is 'Dall'opaco'. This is not a work of fiction, but a discourse with which the author's hypothetical original/primitive ego describes the form of the world.

The initial hypothesis is not so much the initial condition as seen in 'Se allora mi avessero domandato che forma ha il mondo' (*Romanzi e racconti* III, 89), as the unity of the ego, the identity of the consciousness which brings about the synthesis of the perceptions. Therefore the reply to the question formulated in the present remains the same, 'e così anche adesso se mi chiedono che forma ha il mondo', that is, the presence of an ego 'che abita all'interno di me' (*Romanzi e racconti* III, 89). It is through this supertemporal ego that Calvino proposes to describe the form of the world.

The decision to describe the bay of Sanremo, not specified in the text just as the speaker is symmetrically anonymous, clearly answers a logical need, in so far as that landscape is the first image which the ego retains, the one from which all others derive. The problem is that even the first image is actually made up of successive states — not because the ego changes, but because the form of the world varies over time. Thus the form of the world cannot but change continually, and the ego which perceives it is obliged to provide not a single image of it, frozen at the fleeting instant of perception, but a whole series of superimposed snapshots which take in the whole process. All the representations have to be referred to the ego as to a single centre of reference, and that centre of reference must be motionless: in its successive stages of perception, the ego is motionless like the draughtsman's graticule. The eye of the describing ego, like the draughtsman's pencil, moves within this fixed framework following

[17] See 'Il modello dei modelli' in *Palomar*: 'In tutto questo, non che Palomar elaborasse lui stesso dei modelli o s'adoperasse ad applicarne dei già elaborati: egli si limitava a immaginare un giusto uso di giusti modelli per colmare l'abisso che vedeva spalancarsi sempre di più tra la realtà e i principî. Insomma, il modo in cui i modelli potevano essere manovrati e gestiti non entrava nelle sue competenze né nelle sue possibilità di intervento. Di queste cose s'occupavano abitualmente persone molto diverse da lui, che ne giudicavano la funzionalità secondo altri criteri: come strumenti di potere, soprattutto, più che secondo i principî o le conseguenze nella vita della gente. Cosa questa abbastanza naturale, dato che ciò che i modelli cercano di modellare è pur sempre un sistema di potere; ma se l'efficacia del sistema si misura sulla sua invulnerabilità e capacità di durare, il modello diventa una specie di fortezza le cui spesse mura nascondono quello che c'è fuori' (*Romanzi e racconti* II, 966). The underlining is mine.

the outlines of the object to be reproduced in an increasingly detailed analysis until it has to be broken off, not because there are no further details, but because, looked at generally, the overall view has changed and it becomes necessary to start all over again:

> per chi osserva da fermo il mondo si sfalda discontinuo alla vista e all'udito nella frana dello spazio e del tempo
>
> (*Romanzi e racconti* III, 96)

A faithful representation of the world cannot but take account of this discontinuity and for once (and once only, as far as I have been able to ascertain), Calvino does not completely comply with the conventional rules of layout, and uses an unconventional spacing, skipping a line and beginning a new line. But this casual approach is far from being unintentional: on either side of the blank lines are a total of forty 'paragraphs' which subdivide the discourse, and they follow the narrowing down of attention from the world to the ego.

'Dall'opaco' is the most exhaustive of the descriptions Calvino has given us of Sanremo framed by a visual angle which seems to correspond to that of 'Uomo nei gerbidi'. From some fixed but indeterminate point on the hills, the descriptive device rotates to survey all directions before it; it uses different lenses for near and far, has a memory of what these places were like in the past, is able to register sounds and to regret the fact that only at night are they proportionate to the distances from which they come. Further, it is endowed with a stroboscopic device with which it studies the rotation of shadows around objects, and even has an economic intelligence which allows it to make profit correspond to desire for sun: in short, the apotheosis of hyper-realism.

However, this being Calvino, the apotheosis is in the negative. The inner panorama attains a maximum of density and is continually crumbling, fragmented, dissolved. The perfection of the mechanism is continually thwarted by the presence of new obstacles: from a point with maximum visibility objects cannot be seen in their entirety; whatever line one tries to follow — with the exception of the line between sea and sky, which we already know to be illusory — will inevitably end in the void. Furthermore, after having positioned itself to the south and turned towards the sea, the Calvinian ego begins to seek out the opaque, what is behind it and which it cannot see so well, what cannot be seen because it is beyond the horizon, in short everything which is outside the frame.

Here, I believe, we have the same desire for flight which appears in 'Il conte di Montecristo', and as the possible escape which Dantès tries to contemplate is left as a question mark which will give rise to 'un Montecristo col segno meno' (*Romanzi e racconti* II, 355), the opaque is defined as the reverse side of the world:

> Solo al fondo dei torrenti irti di canne dal frusciare cartaceo, o nelle valli che s'inarcano a gomito, o dietro i cocuzzoli protuberanti sui poggi, e più indietro nel succedersi di contrafforti della catena montagnosa parallela alla costa, si dà quell'incupirsi del verde, quell'affiorare di rocce dalla terra dilavata, quella vicinanza del freddo che sale da sottoterra e lontananza non solo dal mare invisibile ma anche dal feroce azzurro del cielo incombente, quel senso d'un misterioso confine che separa dal mondo aperto ed estraneo, che è il senso d'essere entrati 'int'ubagu' nell'opaco rovescio del mondo

> di modo che potrei definire l''ubagu' come annuncio che il mondo che sto descrivendo ha un rovescio, una possibilità di trovarmi diversamente disposto e orientato, in un diverso rapporto col corso del sole e le dimensioni dello spazio infinito, segno che il mondo presuppone un resto del mondo
>
> (*Romanzi e racconti* III, 99)

The opaque, the reverse side of the world, the elsewhere, represent the non-present and the possible. If the 'aprico' is the past, describable and real, the 'opaco' is the future, which can at most be hypothesized and conjectured about.[18] But the conflict between the two exists from the start:

> e se partendo da quella posizione iniziale considero le fasi successive dello stesso me stesso, ogni passo in avanti può essere pure un ritrarsi, la linea che traccio s'avvolge sempre più nell'opaco, ed è inutile che cerchi di ricordare a che punto sono entrato nell'ombra, già c'ero fin dal principio, è inutile che cerchi in fondo all'opaco uno sbocco all'opaco, ora so che il mondo che esiste è l'opaco e l'aprico ne è solo il rovescio, l'aprico che opacamente si sforza di moltiplicare se stesso ma moltiplica solo il rovescio del proprio rovescio
>
> (*Romanzi e racconti* III, 101)

Understanding the discourse as a description of the thinking ego in time and space, the impossibility of defining the direction of thought will come as no surprise; in relation to the eternity of the present moment, past and future are points on a line which can close in on itself in a circle. But at this point the 'aprico' seems to indicate the world and the 'opaco' the thinking ego:

> 'D'int'ubagu', dal fondo dell'opaco io scrivo, ricostruendo la mappa d'un aprico che è solo un inverificabile assioma per i calcoli della memoria, il luogo geometrico dell'io di un me stesso di cui il me stesso ha bisogno per sapersi me stesso, l'io che serve solo perché il mondo riceva continuamente notizie dell'esistenza del mondo, un congegno di cui il mondo dispone per sapere se c'è.
>
> (*Romanzi e racconti* III, 101)

Basically the argument goes back to Kant, but this work suggests a further development which is better explained in a passage of Palomar:

> Ma come si fa a guardare qualcosa lasciando da parte l'io? Di chi sono gli occhi che guardano? Di solito si pensa che l'io sia uno che sta affacciato ai propri occhi come al

[18] See 'The gap between past and future: the *nunc stans*', in H. Arendt, *The Life of the Mind* (London, Martin and Warburg Ltd, 1978), pp. 202–13. To represent the temporal perception of the thinking ego Arendt interprets and comments upon a text by Kafka as follows: 'It analyses poetically our "inner state" in regard to time, of which we are aware when we have withdrawn from the appearances and find our mental activities recoiling characteristically upon themselves — *cogito me cogitare, volo me velle*, and so on. The inner time sensation arises when we are not entirely absorbed by the absent non-visibles we are thinking about but begin to direct our attention onto the activity itself. In this situation past and future are equally present precisely because they are equally absent from our sense; thus the no-longer of the past is transformed by virtue of the spacial metaphor into something "behind" us and the not-yet of the future into something that "approaches" us from ahead (The German *Zukunft* like the French *avenir*, means, literally What comes toward)', H. Arendt, *The Life of the Mind* (London, Martin and Warburg Ltd, 1978), p. 202. See also above Chapter I, note 20.

> davanzale di una finestra e guarda il mondo che si distende in tutta la sua vastità lì davanti a lui. Dunque: c'é una finestra che si affaccia sul mondo; e di qua? Sempre il mondo: cos'altro volete che ci sia? Con un piccolo sforzo di concentrazione Palomar riesce a spostare il mondo da lì davanti e a sistemarlo affacciato al davanzale. Allora, fuori dalla finestra, cosa rimane? Il mondo anche lì, che per l'occasione s'è sdoppiato in mondo che guarda e mondo che è guardato. E lui, detto anche 'io', cioè il signor Palomar? Non è anche lui un pezzo di mondo che sta guardando un altro pezzo di mondo? Oppure, dato che c'è mondo di qua e mondo di là della finestra, forse l'io non è altro che la finestra attraverso la quale il mondo guarda il mondo. Per guardare se stesso il mondo ha bisogno degli occhi (e degli occhiali) del signor Palomar.
>
> (*Romanzi e racconti* II, 968–69)

The identity, or at least the interdependence, between subject and object, between ego and world, establishes an equivalent identity on the page between those aesthetic categories known as form and content. Landscape description and philosophical argument are interrupted and retraced in ways which may possibly be intended to reproduce the comings and goings of the eye along 'linee spezzate e oblique con segmenti che tendono a sporgere fuori dagli angoli di ogni gradino, come fanno le agavi che crescono spesso sul ciglio' (*Romanzi e racconti* III, 89–90).[19] Just as the landscape is completely in the open, incapable of containing interiors, so too the ego is denied any form of intimist dimension; to explain itself and tell of the interior, it needs to represent the exterior: 'la finestra inquadra il comò con lo specchio su cui passa una nuvola' (*Romanzi e racconti* III, 94). Similarly the discontinuity of the gaze, which can wander freely and yet 'é frantumato tra piani e distanze diverse' (*Romanzi e racconti* III, 94) screened by partial obstacles, imposes upon sight a continual association of incongruous elements:

> le palme si aprono e si chiudono come un ventaglio sulle alberature delle barche da pesca, s'alza il getto di una manica e innaffia un campo di invisibili anemoni.
>
> (*Romanzi e racconti* III, 94)

Even dimensions appear weird: 'mezzo autobus svolta nella mezza curva della carrozzabile e sparisce tra le spade dell'agave' (*Romanzi e racconti* III, 94) in an associative gymnastics which seems spontaneously to generate that play of combinations characteristic of Calvino's story-telling. We are even given exercises of narrative fantasy, possible plots sketched in a few lines:

> la nave che vedo prendere il largo e sparire nel riflesso del sole, approderà a porti opachi, vedrà spalti grigi di moli affiorare da un mattino di nebbia, le luci ancora accese dei docks
>
> (*Romanzi e racconti* III, 100)

19 See Montale, 'L'agave sullo scoglio' and 'Riviere' in *Ossi di seppia* (Milan, Mondadori, 1948), pp. 101 and 139–41 (p. 139). The latter is also quoted by Calvino in 'Liguria': 'Nei superstiti giardini le palme continuano ad agitare le loro foglie al vento, l'agave ad affacciare le sue foglie carnose ed acuminate sulla costa scoscesa («gli stocchi d'erbaspada penduli da un ciglione» d'una poesia di Eugenio Montale)' (*Saggi* II, 2383–84). The underlining is mine to stress the link with the section 'Sporgendosi dalla costa scoscesa' in *Se una notte d'inverno un viaggiatore*.

while, conversely, 'Il cacciatore che risale la mulattiera nel gerbido' will manage to 'scorgere una thule dalle porte dorate, una helsinki con la sua bianca piazza, città aprica su un golfo di ghiaccio' (*Romanzi e racconti* III, 100).

To conclude, the answer to the philosophical question of the form of the world coincides with a stylistic self-portrait.

Le città invisibili

The interview with Maria Corti already quoted (1985, see p. 7 above) vouches for the presence of the Sanremo landscape in *Le città invisibili*, but a key passage is to be found at the beginning of the sixth dialogue when the Khan, for once leaving the imperial residence, takes Marco to visit the old Quimsai district and asks him if he has ever seen anything like it. Although the description of the city in which they find themselves leaves no room for doubt (it is Venice, and certainly not the lost Quinsai), Marco's reply is, surprisingly, in the negative. We have no doubts about the fact that Marco is lying: he avoids Kublai's eye and bows his head. No less disoriented than the emperor of the Tartars, the reader must wait for night to fall in the story, and for the questioning of the merchant to run its course until all the cities known to him have been exhausted. And now at last the emperor asks him about Venice, the only city he has never heard of. Marco retorts that he has been talking of nowhere else and although, as the Khan points out, he has never mentioned it by name, Venice is the 'implicit' city, the one in comparison with which all other cities assume their own characteristics. The Khan would like to force him to begin to describe Venice in its entirety and then tell of other cities independently of the memory of Venice, but Marco replies:

> — *Le immagini della memoria, una volta fissate con le parole, si cancellano,* — *disse Polo.* — *Forse Venezia ho paura di perderla tutta in una volta, se ne parlo. O forse, parlando d'altre città, l'ho già perduta a poco a poco.*
>
> (*Romanzi e racconti* II, 432)

This observation is not limited to the relation between Marco and Venice, but also applies to that between Calvino and Sanremo; indeed the reflective play between the author who manages not to name it, and the character whose intentional omission, or lie, it underlines, becomes charged with symbolic pathos. And here we have the procedure or expedient of the revealing and concealing of the Sanremo landscape contained in the descriptive metaphor which precedes Marco's words:

> *L'acqua del lago era appena increspata; il riflesso di rame dell'antica reggia dei Sung si frantumava in riverberi scintillanti come foglie che galleggiano.*
>
> (*Romanzi e racconti* II, 432)

where the image is viewed not in its entirety, but broken up, transformed by a simile, and reflected. Basically, we already know about this reflection: the writer is not striving for a representation of reality, but for the representation of a reality limited to the inner dimension. The breaking down, on the other hand, may be seen as a procedure which, beyond its undoubted negative implications — in this case, perhaps, the absence of a complete description of the hypothetical palace lit by the rays of the rising sun — also offers positive ones, here 'l'effetto brezza', both clear and implicit.

> Il mio libro in cui credo d'avere detto più cose resta *Le città invisibili*, perché ho potuto concentrare su un unico simbolo tutte le mie riflessioni, le mie esperienze, le mie congetture; e perché ho costruito una struttura sfaccettata in cui ogni breve testo sta vicino agli altri in una successione che non implica una consequenzialità o una gerarchia ma una rete entro la quale si possono tracciare molteplici percorsi e ricavare conclusioni plurime e ramificate.
>
> (*Saggi* I, 689–90)

This statement, contained in the *Lezioni americane*, makes it possible to choose a route which (though it will not include the word Sanremo or Riviera di Ponente), does proceed from the 'name', which is also the title of one of the sections of the book. Of the five cities which make it up, it is the third, and thus the central one, Pirra — an intentional homage to a mythical progenitrix of humanity — which provides the most recognizable portrait of Sanremo, because it has two faces. There can be no doubt as to the view of the city described in the words of one who knows it only by hearsay:

> A lungo Pirra è stata per me una città incastellata sulle pendici d'un golfo, con finestre alte e torri, chiusa come una coppa, con al centro una piazza profonda come un pozzo e con un pozzo al centro.
>
> (*Romanzi e racconti* II, 437)

While we do not know whether the information concerning the city after the arrival at Pirra corresponds to the truth, it works for Sanremo,

> [...] e io credevo d'avere sempre saputo che il mare non è in vista della città, nascosto da una duna della costa bassa e ondulata; che le vie corrono lunghe e diritte; che le case sono raggruppate a intervalli, non alte [...]
>
> (*Romanzi e racconti* II, 437)

even if we sense that the low houses are those of the Ligurian town at the time of Calvino's childhood, and if we smile at the almost certain mendacity of 'credevo d'avere sempre saputo', we must resign ourselves to uncertainty.[20] In essence our problem is similar to Marco's:

> Anche la città alta sul golfo è sempre là, con la piazza chiusa intorno al pozzo, ma non posso più chiamarla con un nome, né ricordare come potevo darle un nome che significa tutt'altro.
>
> (*Romanzi e racconti* II, 437)

A non-communicable name, whose meaning varies according to occasion and individual experience, would make no sense on an inner map. Again, the missing name, the name of the real, known city, which does not correspond to its image, refers us to Aglaura, a city on whose qualities there exists a pre-established discourse which, according to Marco, does not correspond to what he himself has seen, 'una città sbiadita, senza carattere, messa lì come

20 See I. Calvino, 'Riviera di Ponente', *Il Politecnico*, 21, 16 February 1946: 'E scendendo si continuano a vedere fasce, cunette e vasche per l'acqua, e poi ancora paesi, sempre grigi e ammucchiati. Uscendo da una 'rivolta' vedi che c'è il mare lì sotto, e alberghi e ville e autobus: solo allora ti accorgi che sei arrivato alla costa'. The historical San Remo is described as 'un agglomerato di case a mezza-costa' in the same issue of the 'Politecnico'.

vien viene' yet nonetheless 'a certe ore, in certi scorci di strade, vedi aprirtisi davanti il sospetto di qualcosa d'inconfondibile, di raro, magari di magnifico', a place which 'vorresti dire cos'è, ma tutto quello che s'è detto finora d'Aglaura imprigiona le parole e t'obbliga a ridire anziché a dire' (*Romanzi e racconti* II, 413). Furthermore, if the discourse woven firmly around Aglaura is false, there is not, and cannot be, a true one:

> E anche a me che vorrei tenere distinte nella memoria le due città, non resta che parlarti dell'una, perché il ricordo dell'altra, mancando di parole per fissarlo, s'è disperso.
>
> (*Romanzi e racconti* II, 414)

The crossroads indicates two equally impossible routes. If, as Freud maintained, 'memory consists of a continual process of transcription,' (Freud 1925, p. 427)[21] and the path to be taken is that of permutation, one will arrive at Clarice, whose successive reworkings, aimed at rethinking and reusing the vestiges of an uncertain past in accordance with the needs of the moment, succeed only in destroying them, effacing their value. (Thus the city which at the start was described as 'glorious' is transformed into its opposite: 'Forse Clarice è sempre stata solo un tramestio di carabattole sbrecciate, male assortite, fuori uso', *Romanzi e racconti* II, 451.)

If, on the other hand, memory is a reservoir of images 'fissate con le parole' once and for all, the goal of the journey stops at self-quotation:

> Irene é la città che si vede a sporgersi dal ciglio dell'altipiano nell'ora che le luci si accendono e per l'aria limpida si distingue laggiù in fondo la rosa dell'abitato: dove é più densa di finestre, dove si dirada in viottoli appena illuminati, dove ammassa ombre di giardini, dove innalza torri con i fuochi dei segnali; e se la sera é brumosa uno sfumato chiarore si gonfia come una spugna lattiginosa al piede dei calanchi.
>
> (*Romanzi e racconti* II, 463)

One omission — the sea — and two variants — artificial light rather than that of the sun, and the possible mist — distinguish the invisible city from its sister-city at the beginning of *Il sentiero dei nidi di ragno* and of 'Uomo nei gerbidi', but the crucial point is that the distance between the observer and the space described has become unbridgeable. And this makes return not only undesired: 'Non che [quelli che la guardano] abbiano intenzione d'andarci — e comunque le strade che calano a valle sono cattive — [...]' but impossible: 'Irene è un nome di città vista da lontano, e se ci si avvicina cambia' (*Romanzi e racconti* II, 463).[22]

[21] S. Freud, 'A note upon the Mystic Writing Pad' (1925 [1924]), in *On Metapsychology. The theory of Psychoanalysis* (Harmondsworth, Middlesex, Penguin Books, Pelikan Freud Library, 1985), Vol. 11, 427–34 (p. 427).

[22] It should however be noted that the affected lack of interest is described in the *Prefazione* 1964 al *Sentiero dei nidi di ragno*, as an irreparable and painful loss: 'il primo libro diventa subito un diaframma tra te e l'esperienza, taglia il fili che ti legano ai fatti, brucia il tesoro di memoria [...] Di questa violenza che le hai fatto scrivendo, la memoria non si riavrà più: le immagini privilegiate resteranno bruciate dalla precoce promozione a motivi letterari, mentre le immagini che hai voluto tenere in serbo, magari con la segreta intenzione di servirtene per opere future, deperiranno, perché tagliate fuori dall'integrità naturale della memoria fluida e vivente. La proiezione letteraria dove tutto è solido e fissato una volta per tutte, ha ormai

Calvino makes an exceptional narrative swerve to emphasize this distance, and while in the descriptive chapters it is presumably to Marco that he entrusts the role of the first-person narrator and to Kublai that of recipient (silent, like the reader), for once he has them both appear together (as in the dialogue in italics) so that we pass from the immediacy of the present declarative to the static atemporality of the narrative present. At the end, the image of Irene has faded and in its place we hear the peremptory words of an ego which, no longer attributable to Marco, is faceless, a mere 'voice off':

> La città per chi passa senza entrarci è una, e un'altra per chi ne è preso e non ne esce; una è la città in cui s'arriva la prima volta, un'altra quella che si lascia per non tornare; ognuna merita un nome diverso; *forse di Irene ho già parlato sotto altri nomi; forse non ho parlato che di Irene.*
>
> (*Romanzi e racconti* II, 463–64, my emphasis)

Marco's words on Venice would seem to have completed a vicious circle and returned to their starting-place.[23] What we have here is not a circle, but perhaps a spiral, because there is still one direction in which to look in the metaphor of waste with which Clarice ended, Clarice a city whose 'regola è mescolarli [i pezzi che la compongono] ogni volta e riprovare

occupato il campo, ha fatto sbiadire, ha schiacciato la vegetazione dei ricordi in cui la vita dell'albero e quella del filo d'erba si condizionano a vicenda. La memoria — o meglio l'esperienza, che è la memoria più la ferita che ti ha lasciato, più il cambiamento che ha portato in te e che ti ha fatto diverso —, l'esperienza primo nutrimento, anche dell'opera letteraria (ma non solo di quella), ricchezza vera dello scrittore (ma non solo di lui), ecco che appena ha dato forma a un'opera letteraria insecchisce, si distrugge. Lo scrittore si ritrova ad essere il più povero degli uomini. [...] Un libro scritto non mi consolerà mai di tutto ciò che ho distrutto scrivendolo' (*Romanzi e racconti* I, 1203–04). Furthermore this passage seems to me to contain also an explanation for the motif of distance and fog which characterizes Irene in *Le città invisibili, Romanzi e racconti* II, 463–64. 'Così mi guardo indietro [...] e tutto è lontano e nebbioso' (*Romanzi e racconti* I, 1203–04).

23 Though it may be useful to conclude the matter of the name of Sanremo by observing that in his other works too Calvino kept to the unwritten rule of avoiding uttering it (and the omissions which appear most obvious concern the 'realist' writings we have considered in the first part of this research). Thus a paragraph in '*La poubelle agréée*' strikes me as all the more exceptional: 'Risalendo più in là nella memoria affiora la San Remo dell'infanzia, ed ecco lo spazzino col sacco sulle spalle venirsene a piedi su per i tornanti del viale fino alla villa, a raccogliere i rifiuti dal bidone di zinco: la vita signorile sembrava garantita in eterno dalla disponibilità di mano d'opera e dai bassi salari' (*Romanzi e racconti* III, 62–63). Here childhood and considerations of an economic order are closely intertwined and create the impression of a guilty Eden, where the only possibility of redemption seems to be (as in fairy-tales) in the transformation of the narrator into a roadsweeper, which does indeed partially happen, in that the narrating ego is responsible for the removal of rubbish (though only for his own family). Consideration of 'La poubelle agréée' is germane to my argument, because of its closeness, and in a sense its complementarity, to the theme that is the object of study in *Le città invisibili* (chronologically, too, as stated in the text itself (*Romanzi e racconti* III, 79). The subject is disposal as relationship between the individual and the society in which he lives, rendered in mimetic style (low-mimetic or comic, one might even say, given the initial anti-climax: 'Delle faccende domestiche, l'unica che io disimpegni con qualche competenza e soddisfazione è quella di mettere fuori l'immondizia' (*Romanzi e racconti* III, 59), and limited, at least at first, to the implicit rules and rituals which govern the disposal of rubbish); but the ending brings the hidden theme to the surface — namely, that of writing as a transformation of thought and memory from private to public material, with the inevitable conclusion that: 'Scrivere è dispossessarsi non meno che il buttar via, è allontanare da me un mucchio di fogli appallottolati e una pila di fogli scritti fino in fondo, gli uni e gli altri non più miei, deposti, espulsi' (*Romanzi e racconti* III, 79).

a metterli insieme' and which, to judge by the Khan's observations, is not very different from Marco's descriptive procedure:

> Kublai Khan s'era accorto che le città di Marco Polo s'assomigliavano, come se il passaggio dall'una all'altra, non implicasse un viaggio, ma uno scambio d'elementi.
>
> (*Romanzi e racconti* II, 391)

The combinatory rule followed by both Marco's descriptions and the transformations of Clarice, is not arbitrary: it is dictated by reasons, possibly secret and inscrutable, but which can be seen as deriving from an inner perspective (as in the orientalizing fable which concludes the fifth series); while the 'città a scale, esposta a scirocco, su un golfo a mezzaluna [...]' (*Romanzi e racconti* II, 391), hypothesized about in the abstract by the Khan, is declared to be non-existent. We may note that the first words describing this non-existent city at least indicate Sanremo, though its gratuitous evocation, like the dreams of the Khan, 'opera della mente e del caso' (*Romanzi e racconti* II, 392), exclude it, according to Marco, from the imaginable cities. Thus for cities, as for dreams, Marco seems to be saying that it is desire or fear which inspire the laws which keep them together and make their description possible (*Romanzi e racconti* II, 391–92).

The subtle arabesque which links Marco's discourse and the stratifications of Clarice is the balance between desire and fear, between worth and wastage, between the positive and negative aspects which symmetrically dominate the opening and closing *cornici* of the book. It is also an insoluble equation, which cannot be reduced to zero, just as the Khan's empire, reduced to a square of the chessboard, is still just a piece of wood, cut from a particular tree, in the vastness of a forest which, however far away and unknown, is still part of the Khan's empire. Here too we may sense an autobiographical implication in that the woods to which Marco alludes may be related to the trees which surrounded the distant Sanremo villa, and the scientific description of buds and frosts and pruning which he proffers so knowledgeably, may be another tribute to the author's botanically-inclined parents, and the memory of a lesson learned during childhood.

Balance is probably one of the book's basic characteristics: not just in terms of its geometrical structure, but also, and perhaps above all, in the relationship between what is said and not said, what is written and what is hidden in the writing itself. Although often intentionally contradictory, the *cornici* allude on several occasions to preverbal communication between Marco and Kublai:

> *Ma ciò che rendeva prezioso a Kublai ogni fatto o notizia riferito dal suo inarticolato informatore era lo spazio che restava loro intorno,* un vuoto non riempito di parole. *Le descrizioni di città visitate da Marco Polo avevano questa dote: che ci si poteva girare in mezzo col pensiero, perdercisi, fermarsi a prendere il fresco, o scappare via di corsa.*
>
> (*Romanzi e racconti* II, 386, my emphasis)

Clearly, this is a silence capable of triggering off an imaginative mechanism, a spacing of discourse which is filled up only according to the needs and availability of the recipient — that is, once again, his desires and fears — an act of speech dictated not by the voice, but by the ear (*Romanzi e racconti* II, 473). It is up to the reader to decide what to make of the allusions which the text contains as the occasion arises, choosing which should be seen in relation to other sections of the text and which should be placed in the wider context of the author's work, as for example the metaphor of Marco's imprisonment,

> *altra ancora quella* [la descrizione del mondo] *che potrei dettare in tarda età, se venissi fatto prigioniero da pirati genovesi e messo in ceppi nella stessa cella con uno scrivano di romanzi d'avventura.*
>
> (*Romanzi e racconti* II, 473)

which refers both to the historical information on the character and the composition of *Il milione*, and to 'Il conte di Montecristo'.

Se una notte d'inverno un viaggiatore

The pattern sea–city–hills reappears for the last time in Calvino's work in *Se una notte d'inverno un viaggiatore*. It is connected mainly with Pëtkwo, the seaside resort where the diarist, the narrator of the third novelistic incipit entitled 'Sporgendosi dalla costa scoscesa', is staying. But the Ligurian landscape has undergone such alteration and camouflage — for instance the shift of light and colour towards violet, the constant reference to the harshness of the climate, the replacement of the Mediterranean deckchair with covered wicker armchairs typical of Northern countries, as beach furniture — that it might have seemed more apt to consider it in the earlier section together with *Il barone rampante* and *La speculazione edilizia*. All the more so in that one might well maintain that here it is only one detail of the whole — the geographical orientation or the transposition of latitude — which brings about the transformation of the whole. Nonetheless, it differs in certain important respects from the works of the previous section: first, whereas, in the former, it might be said to be precisely the detail in question (trees, or rather love of trees; ants, concrete, or rather the loathing of ants and concrete) which generated the plot, the transposition of latitude is completely incidental to the plot of 'Sporgendosi della costa scoscesa' (microplot) and serves rather to link it to the previous incipit and hence to the general narrative framework (macroplot). Secondly, the peculiarity of this narrative is the introduction of a cluster of emblems, each already amply elaborated and exploited by Calvino, such as the shell, the weather station and the prison, clearly used both as evident self-quotation and as generators of the plot.[24] That is: beyond this masking, elements of the re-elaboration of previous literary material come into play, but these seem to me closer in spirit, or in terms of compositional sophistication, to the works studied in this chapter than to those of the previous one.

In the general scheme of *Se una notte d'inverno un viaggiatore* which Calvino published in *Alfabeta* (1979), 'Sporgendosi della costa scoscesa' is described as a 'romanzo simbolico-interpretativo'. Indeed the narrator is immediately presented as a subject exaggeratedly interested in the analysis of everyday events not as such, but as symbolic indicators provided

24 It should be noted that the possibility of a different orientation was already contemplated in 'Dall'opaco', however in that case it referred to the ego rather than to the world (*Romanzi e racconti* III, 99). See also above p. 85. World-rotation will come rather naturally to Palomar and will only require a little effort of concentration on his part (*Romanzi e racconti* II, 969). See also above, pp. 86–87.

by the world for the ego. The minuteness with which he looks at the world links him with other narrator-observers, even if here the caricatural aspects are heavily emphasized, and both the reference to convalescence from an unspecified illness, and the implications of unsociability and sexual repression, help to instil in the reader a sardonic distrust vis-à-vis his powers of judgement. The conclusion of the story will see him suddenly caught up in a network which the reader has been allowed to sense for some time. Even though here he is not a child, we are again in the presence of a naive narrator-observer whose diary has the function of registering both the events he witnesses and the daily conjectures he weaves around them.

The methodical manner in which these daily events are reported creates an analogy between the narrative framework and the first symbol to appear on the scene, namely the weather-station, introduced by the emphatic, and apocalyptic, consideration that:

> Se la fine del mondo si potesse localizzare in un punto preciso, questo sarebbe l'osservatorio metereologico di Pëtkwo.
>
> (*Romanzi e racconti* II, 663)

This comment clearly characterizes the diarist rather than the place described — as he will say later, 'un'inclinazione naturale mi porta a riconoscere i miei stati d'animo nell'immobile sofferenza delle cose' (*Romanzi e racconti* II, 670) reinforcing the reader's detachment from a narrator who is presented as emotionally fragile. But the main attribute of the weather-station, too, is fragility: metal roofing held in place by 'quattro pali di legno un po' traballanti, una fragile attrezzatura', a complex

> che isolato sul ciglio d'una scarpata del giardino municipale [...] sembra una trappola per cicloni, un'esca messa lì per attirare le trombe d'aria [...] offrendosi già come relitto ideale alla furia degli uragani.
>
> (*Romanzi e racconti* II, 662)

The weather-station is linked to the figure of the meteorologist signor Kauderer, of whom it is said

> Mi sono reso conto che la presenza del signor Kauderer è importante per me: il fatto che qualcuno dimostri ancora tanto scrupolo e metodica attenzione, anche se so bene che tutto è inutile, ha su di me un effetto tranquillizzante, forse perché viene a compensare il mio modo di vivere impreciso, che — malgrado le conclusioni cui sono giunto, — continuo a sentire come una colpa.
>
> (*Romanzi e racconti* II, 666)

Thus the figure of Kauderer is a further embodiment of the unswerving if perennially dissatisfied devotion to professional duty towards which Calvino shows such ambivalence. His treatment is clearly comical: even visually he appears like a vignette from a comic paper of the early years of the century.[25] But he is also put forward, however mockingly, as an

[25] See *Lezioni americane*: 'Il mio mondo immaginario è stato influenzato per prima cosa dalle figure del «Corriere dei Piccoli», allora il più diffuso settimanale italiano per bambini' (*Saggi* I, 708–09). Specifically the figure of Kauderer seems modelled on a quatrain by Vittorio Metz: «Se mi chiamassi Procopio | e fossi senza difetti | mi comprerei un telescopio | ed un vestito a quadretti», quoted by Calvino in the obituary of this illustrator (*Saggi* II, 2900).

embodiment of political engagement, in his clandestine involvement in the project of collective escape, which will be discussed later.

The second symbol to appear is in fact the fortress-prison, interpreted at first in the circumscribed, narcissistic manner of the narrator:

> Oggi ho visto una mano sporgersi da una finestra della prigione, verso mare. [...] Pur sapendo che vi sono rinchiusi i carcerati, ho sempre visto la fortezza come un elemento della natura inerte, del regno minerale. Perciò l'apparizione della mano m'ha stupito come fosse uscita dalla roccia. [...] Per me è stato come un segno che veniva dalla pietra: la pietra voleva avvertirmi che la nostra sostanza era comune e perciò qualcosa di quel che costituisce la mia persona sarebbe rimasto, non si sarebbe perso con la fine del mondo: una comunicazione sarà ancora possibile nel deserto privo di vita, privo della mia vita e d'ogni mio ricordo.
>
> (*Romanzi e racconti* II, 663)

The prison suggests a symbol of something negative and unavoidably physical. From the rest of the story, it seems legitimate to associate the hand protruding from the grating with the imprisoned lover of signorina Zwida, at whom the gesture is probably aimed. What certainly does seem important is the narrator's instinctive identification with the imprisoned man:

> dirò che la mano mi è parsa bianca e sottile, una mano non dissimile dalle mie, in cui nulla indicava la rozzezza che ci s'attende da un galeotto.
>
> (*Romanzi e racconti* II, 663)

This is an identification which, as we have seen, already functions with the other symbols to imply that the scenario of Pètkwo is an inner scenario in which each element, however different it may be, is to be considered as part of the ego. This seems also to be true for signorina Zwida, who first appears as seductively absorbed in drawing shells. Like Kauderer, Zwida too represents an attitude to reality with which the narrator feels uneasy:

> L'applicazione con cui questa ragazza si dedica a disegnare conchiglie indica in lei una ricerca della perfezione come forma che il mondo può e quindi deve raggiungere; io al contrario sono da tempo convinto che la perfezione non si produce che accessoriamente e per caso; quindi non merita interesse alcuno, la natura vera delle cose rivelandosi solo nello sfacelo
>
> (*Romanzi e racconti* II, 665)

Thus the dilemma of which the narrator is a victim may be described as a position of stalemate — imprisonment, perhaps — between the voluntaristic attitude of the one and the optimistic attitude of the other. This is a conjecture which seems justified by the plot's final solution, in which it is Zwida's vitalism which wins over Kauderer's dogmatic rigidity. Just how self-imposed (and ill-conceived) the choice of position of the one is in relation to that of the other, we shall consider further on.

In symmetry with the hand of the invisible convict protruding from a grating in the fortress, the presence of Zwida too is indicated by the fluttering of a lilac ribbon concealed by the curved back of the wicker armchair. Zwida is seated where, a few moments earlier, the diarist had felt a giddy sensation of loneliness:

> Oggi sono arrivato al belvedere sotto al quale si scorge un pezzetto di spiaggia, giù in basso, deserta di fronte al mare grigio. I seggioloni di vimini dalle alte spalliere ricurve, a cesto, per riparare dal vento, disposti in semicerchio, sembravano indicare un mondo in cui il genere umano è scomparso e le cose non sanno che parlare della sua assenza.
>
> (*Romanzi e racconti* II, 663–64)

Thus, right from the start, the presence of Zwida fills a void, satisfying an instinctive desire which is immediately coloured by erotic connotations. In the dream context the shells she draws represent the female genitals, and the possibility of such an allusion is confirmed by the fact that this obvious but restrained symbol is replaced by another, much more explicit one:

> La signorina Zwida stava disegnando un riccio di mare. [...] Il riccio era rovesciato su uno scoglio, aperto: contraeva le spine cercando inutilmente di raddrizzarsi. Il disegno della ragazza era uno studio della polpa umida del mollusco, nel suo dilatarsi e contrarsi, resa in chiaroscuro, e con una tratteggiatura fitta e irta tutt'intorno. [...] Tanto la vista del riccio quanto il disegno trasmettevano sensazioni sgradevoli e crudeli, come un viscere esposto agli sguardi.
>
> (*Romanzi e racconti* II, 667)

The shift from both the surreal lilac ribbon to this description of an upturned sea-urchin give the sense of a dramatic, and regressive, lessening of abstraction. It is true that Calvino continues to express himself through symbols and metaphors, but this is done in conformity with the narrative register of this particular incipit romanzesco and does not apply to the rest of *Se una notte d'inverno un viaggiatore.* What is interesting here is the markedly dream-like character of 'Sporgendosi della costa scoscesa', not just because of the detail, significant in itself, that Zwida claims to be drawing the sea-urchin 'perchè era un'immagine che tornava nei suoi sogni e voleva liberarsene' (*Romanzi e racconti* II, 668), but since the whole narrative mechanism appears to be built up as a collage of dream images re-ordered with the misleading interpretative logic of the narrator, in itself a sort of parody of the dream process. This, it seems to me, is how the descriptive fragments quoted in connection with the prison and the armchairs on the beach, and the diarist's fantasy of satisfying Zwida's request, should be interpreted:

> Vidi me stesso nell'atto di presentarle il grappino di ferro come fosse un mazzo di fiori: l'immagine nella sua incongruità aveva qualcosa di stridente e di feroce. Certo vi si nascondeva un significato che mi sfuggiva; e ripromettendomi di meditarvi sopra con calma risposi di sì.
>
> (*Romanzi e racconti* II, 671)

The grapnel is the key to the story: not only because Zwida's request conceals (though only for the narrator) the plan of escape which will lead to the final loss, but also and above all in that its interpretation casts light upon the dilemma of the protagonist:

> Compresi che l'oggetto racchiudeva un messaggio per me, e dovevo decifrarlo: l'àncora, un'esortazione a fissarmi, ad aggrapparmi, a dar fondo, ponendo fine al mio stato fluttuante, al mio tenermi alla superficie. Ma ques'interpretazione poteva lasciar adito a dubbi: poteva essere pure un invito a salpare, a buttarmi verso il largo.
>
> (*Romanzi e racconti* II, 670)

The indecisive narrator does not clarify what he might cling to, nor in which direction he might put out to sea, because suddenly the grapnel takes on the form of a symbol of a risky emotional investment:

> Qualcosa nella forma del grappino, i quattro denti rincagnati, le quattro braccia di ferro consumate dallo strisciare contro la roccia dei fondali, m'ammonivano che ogni decisione non sarebbe stata senza strappi e sofferenze. A mio sollievo restava il fatto che non si trattava d'una pesante áncora d'alto mare, ma d'un'agile ancoretta: non mi si chiedeva dunque di rinunciare alla disponibilità della giovinezza, ma solo di sostare un momento, di riflettere, di sondare l'oscurità di me stesso.
>
> (*Romanzi e racconti* II, 671)

The diarist substitutes the study of the messages sent him by the surrounding world with that of the messages contained within the ego. The link with reality, already tenuous, is broken and the final catastrophe becomes inevitable. The effect is comical, however, because from the start the author has provided us with sufficient reason to regard the narcissistic daydreaming of the diarist with detachment. Read as a parable, the text of 'Sporgendosi dalla costa scoscesa' once more confirms the triumph of what in Freudian terms one might call the reality principle over the pleasure principle.

But it is an ambiguous confirmation. In *Beyond the Pleasure Principle* (1920) Freud explains the abandoning of the reality principle in terms of instinctual behaviour which masks a desire for self-destruction.[26] Pleasure would thus be a self-destructive challenge to the reality principle: whereas healthy behaviour tries to learn to bear lack of pleasure by appealing to the reality principle, the neurotic deals with it by repeating an earlier painful experience, retracing an infantile, instinctual model.

Thus the text of 'Sporgendosi dalla costa scoscesa' uses a neurotic character-narrator, but a Freudian reading may go further. It may be a new, and is certainly chronologically the last, explanation which the author offers of his desire to bring the landscape of Sanremo on stage again. Freud defines the self-destructive compulsion to repeat as instinctual and, in the same essay, instinct is defined as 'an urge inherent in organic life to restore an earlier state of things' (Freud 1920, p. 308), using an example taken from the behaviour of certain species of fish which lay their eggs in waters remote from their natural habitat and which scientists believe was their original one. It is possible that Calvino would not have objected to a comparison between his own creativity and the behaviour of these species of migratory fish, but the scientific nature of the comparison is not as cheering as it might seem: according to Freud, instinctual life as a whole is destructive.

[26] S. Freud, 'Beyond the Pleasure Principle' (1920), in *On Metapsychology. The Theory of Psychoanalysis* (Harmondsworth, Middlesex, Penguin Books, Pelikan Freud Library, 1985), Vol. 11, 269–338.

> The hypothesis of self-preservative instincts, such as we attribute to all living beings, stands in marked opposition to the idea that instinctual life as a whole serves to bring about death. Seen in this light, the theoretical importance of the instincts of self-preservation, of self-assertion and of mastery greatly diminishes.
>
> (Freud 1920, p. 311)

In 'Sporgendosi dalla costa scoscesa' the topic of death appears twice, as linked to life through an exchange of smells in the description of the inn 'la Stella della Svezia', and in the secret meeting between the diarist and Kauderer in the cemetery. These are the only two night scenes in the diary and in both the diarist is given information which concerns him and which he does not understand: the relationship between Zwida and the convict, and the escape plan. But the night setting is also indicative of a definite link to the macro-plot and the information before and after 'Sporgendosi dalla costa scoscesa'. As Segre explains (1979, p. 184),[27] Cimmeria, the fictitious country of provenance of the author Ukko Ahti, is a borrowing from Homer, corresponding to the region never reached by the sun's rays, where Ulysses meets the shades of the dead, and also from Ovid, here corresponding to the abode of sleep and dreams.

Dreaming takes us back to the Freudian theory of compulsion and repetition and the impossibility of satisfying the tension caused by repressed instinct; a compulsion harmful to the individual, though useful to society:

> What appears in a minority of individuals as an untiring impulsion towards further perfection can easily be understood as a result of the instinctual repression upon which is based all that is most precious in human civilization. The repressed instinct never ceases to strive for complete satisfaction, which would consist in the repetition of a primary experience of satisfaction. No substitutive or reactive formations and no sublimations will suffice to remove the repressed instinct's persisting tension [...] The backward path that leads to complete satisfaction is as a rule obstructed by the resistances which maintain the repressions. So there is no alternative but to advance in the direction in which growth is still free — though with no prospect of bringing the process to a conclusion or of being able to reach the goal.
>
> (Freud 1920, p. 315)

The impossibility of reaching the goal, of arriving at any conclusion, is the central theme of *Se una notte d'inverno un viaggiatore*. From the very first failed attempt we know that the failure will be repeated, as the Reader's prophetic dream tells us:

> Passi una notte agitata, il sonno è un flusso intermittente e ingorgato come la lettura del romanzo, con sogni che ti sembra siano la ripetizione d'un sogno sempre uguale. Lotti coi sogni come con la vita senza senso né forma, cercando un disegno, un percorso che deve pur esserci, come quando si comincia a leggere un libro e non si sa ancora in quale direzione ti porterà. Quello che vorresti è l'aprirsi di uno spazio e

[27] C. Segre, 'Se una notte d'inverno un viaggiatore sognasse un aleph di dieci colori', *Strumenti critici* 2–3 (October 1979), pp. 177–214 (p. 184).

> d'un tempo astratti e assoluti in cui muoverti seguendo una traiettoria esatta e tesa; ma quando ti sembra di riuscirci t'accorgi d'essere fermo, bloccato, costretto a ripetere tutto da capo.
>
> (*Romanzi e racconti* II, 636)

At the end of the novel the invisible design surfaces casually: it is the list of titles which, read one after the other, forms the beginning of a new novel

> *«Se una notte d'inverno un viaggiatore, fuori dell'abitato di Malbork, sporgendosi dalla costa scoscesa senza temere il vento e la vertigine, guarda in basso dove l'ombra s'addensa in una rete di linee che s'allacciano, in una rete di linee che s'intersecano sul tappeto di foglie illuminate dalla luna intorno a una fossa vuota, — Quale storia laggiù attende la fine? — chiede, ansioso d'ascoltare il racconto».*
>
> (*Romanzi e racconti* II, 868)

Once again the new novel opens with a landscape which repeats the pattern of the gulf of Sanremo. This time it is the substitution of the sea with the 'fossa vuota', a metaphor for death as the last and unavoidable goal of the biographical parabola, which confirms the importance of the Freudian interpretation in terms of compulsion and repetition of the recurrence of the landscape.

Bibliography

This bibliography is divided into two sections: the first contains works by Calvino and the second critical works quoted in the body of the book.

Works by Italo Calvino

Books and periodical publications

Whenever it was possible I quoted from:

Romanzi e racconti, edited by C. Milanini, M. Barenghi and B. Falcetto, I, II and III (Milan, Mondadori, 1991, 1992 and 1994).

Saggi, edited by C. Milanini, M. Barenghi and B. Falcetto, I and II (Milan, Mondadori, 1995).

'Riviera di Ponente', *Il Politecnico*, 21, 16 February 1946.

Fiabe italiane raccolte dalla tradizione popolare durante gli ultimi cento anni e trascritte in lingua dai vari dialetti da Italo Calvino, I and II (Turin, Einaudi, 1956).

Sulla fiaba, edited by M. Lavagetto (Turin, Einaudi, 1988).

I libri degli altri. Lettere 1947–1981, edited by G. Tesio (Turin, Einaudi, 1991).

Critical works quoted

Album Calvino, edited by L. Baranelli and E. Ferrero (Milan, Mondadori, 1995).

H. Arendt, *The Life of the Mind* (London, Martin and Warburg Ltd, 1978).

M. Belpoliti, *Storie del visibile: Lettura di Italo Calvino* (Rimini, Luisè, 1990).

C. Benussi, *Introduzione a Calvino* (Bari, Laterza, 1989).

A. Berardinelli, 'Calvino moralista: ovvero, restare sani dopo la fine del mondo', *Diario*, 9 (February 1991), 37–58.

F. Bernardini, *I segni nuovi di Italo Calvino* (Roma, Bulzoni, 1977).

Calvino: la letteratura, la scienza, la città, Acts of the colloquium held in Sanremo in 1986, edited by G. Bertone (Genova, Marietti, 1988).

G. Bertone, *Italo Calvino: Il castello della scrittura* (Turin, Einaudi, 1994).

B. Bettelheim, *The Uses of Enchantment*, 1975 (London, Penguin, 1978).

I. Bezzera Violante, '«La lettura»: Calvino e un'antologia per la scuola media inferiore', in *Calvino e l'editoria*, edited by L. Clerici and B. Falcetto (Milan, Marcos Y Marcos, 1993), pp. 83–94.

G. Bonsaver, *Il mondo scritto: Forme e ideologia nella narrativa di Italo Calvino* (Turin, Tirrenia, 1995).

G. Briganti, L. Trezzani and L. Laureati, *I Bamboccianti* (Roma, Bozzi, 1983).

C. Cases, 'Calvino e il "pathos della distanza"', in *Città aperta*, 7–8 (1958), pp. 33–35 and in *I metodi attuali della critica in Italia*, edited by M. Corti and C. Segre (Turin, Eri/Edizioni Rai Radiotelevisione Italiana, 1970), pp. 53–58.

A. Dolfi, 'Calvino, l'alfabeto e la morte', in *La Gazzetta di Parma*, 19 June 1987, p. 3.

G. Falaschi, *La resistenza armata nella narrativa italiana* (Turin, Einaudi, 1976). Includes a chapter on Calvino, pp. 96–151.

Italo Calvino. Atti del convegno internazionale, Firenze: Palazzo Medici-Riccardi, 26–28 February 1987, edited by G. Falaschi (Milan, Garzanti, 1988).

G. C. Ferretti, *Le capre di Bikini — Calvino giornalista e saggista 1945–1985* (Roma, Editori Riuniti, 1989).

G. C. Ferretti, *Le avventure del lettore: Calvino, Ludmilla e gli altri* (Lecce, Piero Manni 1997).

P. Ferrua, 'Il sostrato sanremese nella narrativa di Italo Calvino', *Italica*, 54 (1977), 367–69.

A. Fletcher, *Allegory: The Theory of a Symbolic Mode* (Ithaca, N.Y., Cornell University Press, 1964). Quoted from the 1982 edition.

S. Freud, *On Metapsychology. The Theory of Psychoanalysis* (Harmondsworth, Middlesex, Penguin Books, Pelikan Freud Library, 1985), Vol. 11. In particular: 'Beyond the Pleasure Principle' (1920), pp. 269–338, and 'A Note upon the Mystic Writing Pad' (1925 [1924]), pp. 427–34.

P. Giovannetti, 'Calvino, la scuola e l'editoria scolastica: l'idillio dimezzato', in *Calvino e l'editoria*, edited by L. Clerici and B. Falcetto (Milan, Marcos Y Marcos, 1993), pp. 35–82.

C. Ginzburg, *Storia notturna. Una decifrazione del sabba* (Turin, Einaudi, 1989).

K. Hume, *Calvino's Fictions: Cogito and Cosmos* (Oxford, Clarendon Press, 1992).

Laplanche and Pontalis, *The Language of Psycho-analysis* (London, The Hogarth Press, 1973).

M. Lavagetto, preface to Italo Calvino, *Sulla fiaba* (Turin, Einaudi, 1988), pp. vii–xxvii.

P. Lejeune, *Le Pacte autobiographique* (Paris, Editions du Seuil, 1975).

G. Lukàcs, *The Meaning of Contemporary Realism* (London, Merlin, 1963).

M. McLaughlin, 'Life and Literature in Calvino's Early Works', *Journal of the Association of Teachers of Italian*, 35 (1982), 45–59.

M. McLaughlin, 'Continuity and Innovation in Calvino's *Palomar*', *Bulletin of the Society for Italian Studies*, 17 (1984), 43–49.

M. McLaughlin, 'Il "Fondo Italo Calvino"', *Autografo*, 17 (1989), 93–103.

M. McLaughlin, 'Calvino's Library: Labyrinth or Laboratory?', in *Italian Storytellers: Essays on Narrative Literature*, edited by E. Haywood and C. O'Cuilleanain (Dublin, Irish Academic Press, 1989).

P. V. Mengaldo, 'L'arco e le pietre' (on Calvino's *Le città invisibili*), in *La tradizione del novecento* (Milan, Feltrinelli, 1975), pp. 406–26.

M. Merleau-Ponty, *Phénoménologie de la perception* (Paris, Gallimard, 1942).

C. Milanini, *L'utopia discontinua: Saggio su Italo Calvino* (Milan, Garzanti, 1990).

E. Mondello, *Italo Calvino* (Pordenone, Edizioni Studio Tesi, 1990).

E. Montale, *Ossi di seppia* (Milan, Mondadori, 1948).

E. Montale, *La bufera e altro* (Milan, Mondadori, 1957).

U. Musarra-Schroeder, *Il labirinto e la rete: percosi moderni e postmoderni nell'opera di Italo Calvino* (Roma, Bulzoni, 1996).

G. Nava, 'La geografia di Calvino', paper delivered at the 'Convegno internazionale di studi sull'opera di Calvino', Florence, 26–28 February 1987.

C. Nocentini, 'Il paesaggio ricorrente nella narrativa di Calvino' in *The Bulletin of the Society for Italian Studies*, 20 (1987), 13–22.

C. Nocentini, 'La San Remo invisibile di Calvino', in *The Italianist*, 9 (1989), 79–88.

C. Nocentini, 'Fiat Pasta: Food in Calvino's narrative', in *Food in Europe*, edited by J. Wilkins (Oxford, Intellect, 1996), pp. 17–27.

C. Nocentini, 'Narrative and Ideological Function of the Narrator in *Il sentiero dei nidi di ragno*', *Forum for Modern Language Studies*, 33, iv (1997), 369–75.

C. Pavese, '*Il sentiero dei nidi di ragno*', in *La letteratura americana e altri saggi* (Turin, Einaudi, 1962), pp. 267–70.

F. Pedriali, 'Più per paura che per gioco?: Three Textual Explorations of Calvino's *Il sentiero dei nidi di ragno*', in *MLR*, 93/1, 1998, 59–70.

G. Pescio-Bottino, *Calvino* (Florence, La nuova Italia, coll. Il Castoro, 1976).

A. Phillips, 'The Telling of Selves', in *On Flirtation* (London, Faber, 1995).

F. Pierangeli, *Italo Calvino: la metamorfosi e l'idea del nulla* (Soveria Mannelli, Rubettino, 1997).

I. Pizzetti, *Libereso: il giardiniere di Calvino* (Padua, Muzzio, 1993).

V. Propp, *Morphology of the Folktale*, 1928. Quoted from Lawrence Scott's English translation, 9th edn (Austin, University of Texas Press, 1986).

M. Quaini, 'La Sanremo di Italo Calvino', in *Italo Calvino la letteratura, la scienza, la città*, edited by G. Bertone, (Genova, Marietti, 1988), pp. 60–66. Acts of the colloquium held in Sanremo in 1986.

L. Re, *Calvino and the Age of Neorealism: Fables of Estrangement* (Stanford California, Stanford University Press, 1990).

F. Ricci, 'The Recovery of Mnemonic Meaning in *L'entrata in guerra*', *The Review of Contemporary Fiction*, 63/4 (Winter 1986), 31–37.

S. Rushdie, *Imaginary Homelands* (London, Granta Books and Viking Penguins, 1991).

C. Segre, 'Se una notte d'inverno un viaggiatore sognasse un aleph di dieci colori', *Strumenti critici* 2–3 (October 1979), 177–214.

C. Segre, *Fuori dal mondo. I modelli nella follia e nelle immagini dell'aldilà* (Turin, Einaudi, 1990).

T. Todorov, *Introduction à la littérature fantastique* (Paris, Editions du Seuil, 1970).

F. Wahl, 'La logica dell'immagine in Calvino', *Il caffé*, 4 (1964), 36–37.

F. Wahl, 'La parola del paesaggio e il paesaggio parlato', paper delivered at the 'Convegno internazionale di studi sull'opera di Calvino', Florence, 26–28 February 1987.

R. Wittkower, *Art and Architecture in Italy 1600–1750* (Pelican, London, 1982).

Critical works consulted

S. M. Adler, *The Writer as Fablemaker* (Kersey Lane Potomac: José Porrua Turanzas, S.A., 1979).

G. Almansi, 'Il mondo binario di Italo Calvino', *Paragone* (August 1971), pp. 95–110.

R. Andrews, 'Italo Calvino', in *Writers and Society in Contemporary Italy*, edited by M. Caesar and P. Hainsworth (Leamington Spa, Berg Publishers, 1984), pp. 259–81.

C. Benedetti, *Pasolini contro Calvino: Per una letteratura impura* (Turin, Bollati Boringhieri, 1998).

C. Benussi, *Scrittori di terra, di mare, di città: Romanzi italiani tra storia e mito* (Milan, Nuova Pratiche, 1998).

I. Bezzera Violante, '«La lettura»: Calvino e un'antologia per la scuola media inferiore' in *Calvino e l'editoria*, edited by L. Clerici and B. Falcetto (Milano, Marcos Y Marcos, 1993), pp. 83–94.

C. Calligaris, *Italo Calvino* (Milano, Mursia, 1973).

Calvino Revisited, edited by F. Ricci (Ottawa, Dovehouse, 1989).

G. M. Carlton, 'The Genesis of Il barone rampante', *Italica*, 3 (Autumn 1984), 194–206.

R. Ceserani, 'Il caso Calvino', in *Raccontare il postmoderno* (Turin, Bollati Boringhieri, 1997), pp. 166–80.

R. Chessa Wright, *La poetica neobarocca* in Calvino (Ravenna, Longo, 1998).

M. Corti, 'Trittico per Calvino', in *Il viaggio testuale* (Turin, Einaudi, 1978), pp. 169–220.

P. Daros, *Italo Calvino* (Paris, Hachette, 1994).

T. De Lauretis, 'Narrative Discourse in Calvino: Praxis or Poiesis?', *PMLA* (May 1975), pp. 14–25.

T. De Lauretis, 'Calvino e la dialettica dei massimi sistemi', in *Italica*, 1 (1976), 57–74.

T. De Lauretis, 'Calvino and the Amazons', in *Technologies of Gender. Essays on Theory, Film, and Fiction* (Bloomington and Indianapolis: Indiana University Press 1987), pp. 97–83.

A. Dolfi, 'L'ultimo Calvino o il labirinto dell'identità', *Italianistica,* 2–3 (May–December 1983), 363–79.

G. Folena, *Tre narratori. Calvino, P. Levi, Parise* (Padua, Liviana, 1989).

J. Gatt-Rutter, 'Calvino Macrocosm: the Politics of Play', in *Writers and Politics in Modern Italy* (London, Hodder and Stoughton, 1978).

P. Giovannetti, 'Calvino, la scuola e l'editoria scolastica: l'idillio dimezzato' in *Calvino e l'editoria,* edited by L. Clerici and B. Falcetto (Milano, Marcos Y Marcos, 1993), pp. 35–82.

G. Gronda, 'Espressione su un racconto semiologico di Italo Calvino', *The Italianist,* 3 (1983), 56–63.

F. Maura, *Italo Calvino: il tema del labirinto da Le Cosmicomiche a Le città invisibili* (Florence, Atheneum, 1998).

M. McLaughlin, *Italo Calvino* (Edinburgh, Edinburgh University Press, 1998).

I. T. Olken, *With Pleated Eye and Garnet Wing: Symmetries of Italo Calvino* (Ann Arbor Mich., University of Michighan Press, 1984).

C. Ossola, 'L'invisibile e il suo "dove": "geografia interiore" di Italo Calvino', *Lettere italiane,* 2 (1987), 220–31.

M. Schneider, 'Calvino at a Crossroads: Il castello dei destini incrociati', *PMLA,* XCV (1980), 73–90.

P. Spriano, 'Un Calvino rivoluzionario', in *Le passioni di un decennio (1946–1956)* (Milan, Garzanti, 1986), pp. 11–32.

C. Varese, 'Una complessa continuità', *La Rassegna della Letteratura Italiana,* vol. nos 1–2 (1980), 252–56.

C. Varese, 'Lettera a Calvino su Palomar', *Otto/Novecento,* 5–6 (September–December 1984), 193–97.

D. Watson, 'Calvino and the Problem of Textual Referentiality', *The Italianist,* 8 (1988), 66–78.

J. R. Woodhouse, *Italo Calvino* (Hull, Hull University Press, 1968).

SPECIAL ISSUES OF PERIODICALS DEVOTED TO ITALO CALVINO

Review of Contemporary Fiction, 6/2 (Summer 1986).

Nuova Corrente, 99 (January–June 1987) and 100 (July–December 1987).

Riga 9: 'Italo Calvino, Enciclopedia: arte scienza e letteratura', edited by M. Belpoliti (Milan, Marcos Y Marcos, 1995).

Index

Apollonio, U. 51
Arbasino, A. 76
Arendt, H. 86
Aristophanes 41

Balzac, H. 63
Baranelli, L. 6
Barenghi, M. 31
Bassani, G. 67
Belpoliti, M. 58
Benedetti, C. 6
Benussi, C. 6, 37
Berardinelli, A. 34, 81
Bernardini, F. 83
Bertone, G. 6, 29, 65
Bezzera Violante, I. 1
Bettelheim, B. 41, 42, 43, 47
Bo, C. 17
Bonsaver, G. 67, 79
Briganti, G. 58

Calvino, M. 37, 44
Cases, C. 21, 54
Cecchi, E. 52
Chagall, M. 67
Chessa Wright, S. 6
Clerici, L. 1
Corti, M. 6, 21, 54, 73, 88
Croce, B. 72

Dante 5, 8, 27, 41
De Monticelli, R. 32
Dian, S. 65
Dolfi, A. 78
Dumas, A. 82, 83, 84

Falaschi, G. 24, 52, 54
Falcetto, B. 1, 16, 22, 28, 31, 51, 53
Ferrero, E. 6
Ferretti, G. C. 34, 81
Ferrua, P. 53

Fiorentino, P. A. 83
Flaubert, G. 77
Fletcher, A. 51
Freud, S. 23, 51, 57, 68, 75, 90, 97, 98, 99

Gentilini, F. 51
Giovannetti, P. 1
Ginzburg, C. 13
Grimm, J. L. K. and W. K. 42
Gordon, R. 6
Guglielmi, L. 53

Haywood, E. 31
Homer 98
Hume, K. 51

Joyce, J. 67
Kafka, F. 52, 53
Kant, E. 86

Lacan, J. 76
Laplanche, J. 75, 76
Laureati, L. 58
Lavagetto, M. 41
Lejeune, P. 73
Leopardi, G. 79
Lukàcs, G. 27, 28

Maquet, A. 83
Mameli Calvino, E. 64, 65
McLaughlin, M. 6, 31, 50
Marco Polo 5
Mastronardi, L. 71
Mengaldo, P. V. 67
Merleau-Ponty, M. 25
Messia, A. 45
Metz, V. 94
Milanini, C. 20, 23, 31, 34, 50, 65, 73, 74, 78, 81
Mondello, E. 6, 65
Montale, E. 3, 7, 11, 29, 87

Monti, A. 74
Mussolini, B. 35

Napoleon 85
Nava, G. 6
Nietzsche, F. 72

O'Cuilleanain, C. 31
Ovid 98

Pavese, C. 3, 20, 22, 23, 24
Pedriali, F. 31
Pescio Bottino, G. 34, 65, 72
Phillips, A. 76
Pizzetti, I. 53, 65
Pontalis, J. B. 75, 76
Propp, V. 40
Proust, M. 68, 75

Quaini, M. 6

Re, L. 23
Ricci, F. 32
Rousseau, J. J. 72
Rushdie, S. 7

Scott, L. 40
Segre, C. 13, 21, 54, 98
Spitzer, L. 76
Stalin, J. 49
Stevenson, R. L. 40

Tesio, G. 50
Todorov, T. 53
Trezzani, L. 58

Van Laer, P. 58
Verga, G. 3, 12
Vittorini, E. 3, 15, 22, 63

Wahl, F. 50, 52
Wittkover, R. 58